Scottish
£5
(17)

Youngest son of a Lieutenant-Colonel in the Cameronians and a Faroese mother, Richard Young - aka 'Siggy' - has spent much of his working life with the Scottish Court Service. During this time he has also forged a fine reputation as an accomplished amateur cricketer and also as a cricket administrator. For nearly forty seasons now he has plied his trade as a skilful left-arm spinner with a number of famous clubs in the west of Scotland, most notably Clydesdale, with whom he won a Scottish Cup medal, GHK, and, latterly, Weirs.

Young's extensive cricketing background and passion for sport, allied to his long career in the processes of the law and an innate capacity for forensic probing, have combined to produce a remarkable work of scholarship, a genuinely iconoclastic piece of assiduous research, which promises to make a significant contribution to the sizeable canon of Scottish sporting and social literature.

Presented in an engaging, eminently readable style, Young's work proves conclusively that for decades we Scots have been harbouring some major illusions about how we brought soccer to the world, and that, contrary to previous thought, the game of association football, both in a parochial Scottish and a wider global context, owes its roots, remarkably, to the cricket players and administrators of the mid and later nineteenth century Scottish Central Belt, crucially fostered and sponsored by the patronage of a number of major landowners and prominent industrialists.

This is serious revisionist history. Cherished myths are debunked. Young's seminal tour de force is a must-read for all with even a passing interest in the origins of Scottish 'fitba' and the social dynamics of nineteenth century industrial Scotland.

D1344319

As the

Willow Vanishes

Richard S Young

Acknowledgements

I have to thank many people for their assistance in providing me with information for this book, but the respective staff at the National Archives, The National Library of Scotland, the Mitchell Library, Strathclyde University Library, Glasgow University Archives and the Melbourne Cricket Club all have to be praised for their contributions.

The past and present clubs of what is now the Western District Cricket Union and their respective members deserve credit for the provision of the many colours that finally paint the landscape of a backdrop to an important story – the as yet unfinished story of nearly two hundred years of adversity to provide the world with so much that has gone unappreciated for far too long.

Special praise has to be given to Michael Clarkson for his rooting out of some of the treasures to be found within. The direction, writing and compilation of this story would not have been possible had it not been for the help of my brother, Eric, and the guidance and insights of our three friends, Frank Johnstone, Sandy Strang and Derek McLean.

The book is dedicated to all involved, past, present and future, in the playing of cricket in the west of Scotland and beyond. The following pages tell the collective history and they should be proud of it.

Finally, I have to thank my wife, Lesley, and my daughter, Freya, for their patience, and their support, in allowing me to realise a life-long ambition – finally getting the story told. Enjoy the read.

Contents

Foreword

Reader, you are in for a treat. And possibly a shock. Richard 'Siggy' Young has just written an astonishing cricket book about football. Or perhaps it's a stunning football book about cricket. One thing's for sure. Make no mistake. It's an utter gem.

The compelling stuff of sporting revelation. Iconoclastic in the extreme. A consummate crucifier of cosy urban myth. A deadly debunker of received wisdoms.

Received wisdom number one states that we Scots have from time immemorial been a football-centric race. Yes, pioneering Scotland can lay compelling claim to being the cradle of association football. Witness this summer's worthy Kelvingrove Museum exhibition orchestrated by the Scottish Football Museum at Hampden entitled 'More Than A Game: How Scotland Shaped World Football'. Yes, too, football has long defined our quintessential sense of Scottishness. Witness that catastrophic 1978 sojourn to Argentina and its extended toxic aftermath: 'It's not that we lost,' opined Willie McIlvanney in 'Surviving The Shipwreck', 'but that it meant so much. Losing a football match shouldn't be confused with loss of identity. I suspect that the kind of commitment Scots invest in football means that there's less left for arguably more important concerns.' But that, argues Young compellingly, is only one small, over-simplified part of a far larger, far more complex and exciting historical jigsaw.

There was much more to the birth and subsequent explosive rise of football in Scotland than mere football. There was cricket. Scottish cricket. Big Scottish cricket.

Received wisdom number two articulates that cricket is a fundamentally English qua English upper-class pursuit. The exclusive preserve and province of Sassenach toffs. Alien to the Scots psyche. Anathema to rugged, hard-wrought Caledonian working-class values. An affront. Not so, postulates Young. The second half of the nineteenth century witnessed the irresistible rise of cricket in industrial Scotland and elsewhere north of the border. Hundreds of teams sprang up. Literally. Cricket in Possil? T20 in Tollcross? You'd better believe it.

And here's the rub. This cricket eruption, Young proves convincingly, was the essential precursor, the crucial sine qua non forerunner, from which our football evolved. Scotland owes its centrality in the birth of fitba almost exclusively to its cricketing roots. Cue the big central-belt landowners, industrialists and financiers. These were the key players, the vital movers and shakers from whose 'Big House Cricket' - echoes here of modern Aussie 'Big Bash'? - the game of football would suddenly emerge, as the later nineteenth century morphed into the twentieth.

Young produces much quality research and startling stats to validate these remarkable claims. And it's all leavened with engaging anecdotal reminiscences from his own life and times as an accomplished cricketer in his own right and an ardent football follower in a later era in his native Glasgow.

In a number of journalistic incarnations over the years as a sports columnist on 'The Scotsman', 'The Edinburgh Evening News', 'The Scotland on Sunday', and 'The Herald', I've enjoyed the pleasure and the privilege to witness first hand many a stirring sporting revelation that quickened the pulse. None more so than now when encountering 'Siggy' Young's thrilling seminal tome. See Scottish football - and cricket - in a dramatically new and revisionist light. Lift the scales from your eyes. Be enlightened. Be enthralled. Read on.......

Sandy Strang
Glasgow
August 2013

Sandy Strang of Clydesdale and Des Walker of Queen's Park with the Scottish Cup ahead of the 100th Cup Final on 18th May 1985 at Hampden Park. Sandy Strang was a Cambridge Blue at Football, played for Queen's Park, was captain of Clydesdale's Cricket and Football Clubs, and has 6 Scottish Cup winners medals at cricket. On 8th September 1985, Sandy was the man of the match in cricket's Scottish Cup Final when Clydesdale defeated Poloc in a derby cup final played at Hamilton Crescent, the scene of the first football international.

Preface

It is late November 2011. The year is coming to its customary halt with the fast approaching festive period. The weather is fairly grim, and on reflection, while staring at my computer, it had been a difficult year for me. To be honest, I was looking forward to the New Year and the fresh hopes that come with it. In Scots colloquial parlance, the perfect word to describe my demeanour would be "scunnered" – thoroughly fed up, disaffected, depressed and disappointed.

In June, I had badly broken my right hand whilst attempting to take a low catch in a cricket cup match and my season had come to an abrupt end with a general anaesthetic operation and four months of sporting an uncomfortable plaster cast. I was annoyed at getting injured and having no participation. The domestic cricket structure in Scotland was at a crossroads with many clubs wanting change. Cricket Scotland, the sport's national governing body, had invited me to join a committee called the Future Structures Group charged with the task of bringing about a change that would be beneficial to the game throughout the land. A summer of meetings and discussions followed and proposals were issued to all the regional leagues and the respective clubs to consider, and in doing so, the feelings of discontent gathered an unprecedented impetus for the delivery of urgent change.

This desire for urgent change had become the major talking point at most clubs, and the press had picked up on the polarised opinions that were appearing in the media and social forums. Instead of correcting the concerns and introducing a structure that was both fair and equitable for all to participate in, the clubs ended up voting in a format that was neither a compromise or even beneficial to the furtherance of cricket at a domestic level.

The sport was in danger of self-destruction as a result of self-interest and petty bickering. A sizeable schism now divided the country into an east/west geography and conflicting ideologies and principles. Only unlikely, unexpected and unprecedented intervention could fill the void and bridge the gulf that existed between Scotland's cricketing regions.

As an escape from this mire of uncertainty, I returned to investigating and researching material for an ongoing hobby project, The Lost Grounds of the West. This project was simply the gathering of snippets of information, stories, photographs, associations, club histories and reminiscences of Glasgow area cricket clubs and revisiting a personal thesis – "Big House" cricket. By doing so previously, I had looked to the past to find answers to the future which in turn had been implemented by the Western District Cricket Union in 2010 in an overhaul by its Reconstruction and Design committee.

This Reconstruction and Design committee had had the perfect opportunity to modernise setup and structure in order to facilitate the strengthening and progression of its clubs with the ultimate aim of promoting to and surviving at the highest level possible of Scottish domestic cricket. The new structure provided a genuine feeder system, a compact route for all clubs to find their correct playing level and was resilient and flexible enough to accommodate any prospective domestic reorganisation in the future.

Was a second look back at the past the answer to solve a current problem?

While conducting this second journey back in time, I had decided to be a bit leftfield and narrowed my search parameters. I typed in "Western cricket + Glasgow 19th Century" and hit the return button and awaited the results.........

I chanced upon a publication that may, in time, become of extreme important historical importance to a nation. The perceptions of the development of cricket in Scotland will certainly be changed and the current Scottish "history" of the game could be faced with a major reconsideration.

"The Laws of Cricket, revised by the Marylebone Club, in the year 1828, observed by the Western Cricket Club of Glasgow, instituted in 1829".

This document sits in the special collections section of the Glasgow University library. It forms part of the David Murray bequeath of 1927 to the University, where his collection of over 15,000 printed books and 200 manuscripts, his own documents and papers, and those of his late father, have been deposited. David Murray (1842-1928) was a Glasgow lawyer, antiquary and bibliographer, and his father, David Murray, was secretary of the first cricket club in Glasgow, the Western Cricket Club.

The document provides the laws for the cricketers of the era to follow but I was not prepared for the ramifications of what else was included within the publication - the membership list.

My original thesis for "Big House" cricket needed a proof to support the theory that cricket's establishment in the west coast had begun with social gatherings and the excitement of gambling, and over time, as the game spread in popularity, the clubs appeared and the sport became developed to what we see today.

But for all of that to happen, there has to be a starting point or creation event. This club, the Western Cricket Club of Glasgow, could be the originator of what we now understand and take for granted. The first step in finding and then following in the footsteps of its founders begins here.

But it isn't just the playing of cricket that's being created. It is much, much more and on a scale that has never been previously considered.

Glasgow's forgotten legacy to the world, through the endeavours of a single sport, can be remembered again.

My dismay of late November 2011 had vanished and my personal quest to find answers to the future by looking at the past was re-invigorated.

A few days after my discovery within the special collections section of the Glasgow University library and following a turbulent summer and autumn of debate and discontent, Cricket Scotland provided the unlikely, unexpected and unprecedented intervention that Scottish domestic cricket so desperately needed. The national governing body in-filled the internecine schism that had appeared, overturned the decisions of the clubs, grabbed them all by the scruff of the neck and gave them a jolly good shake and threw their first teams into a regionalised structure called the Cricket Scotland League.

It is in its early days as a concept and it will be reviewed and changed accordingly, as evidenced by recent developments, but it appears to be a success so far. It has certainly stopped the self-interest and the bickering, but more importantly, it has made many people finally realise that the future survival of their clubs, and the sport in Scotland, depends on them acting as clubs and not simply by playing as teams.

LAWS OF CRICKET,

REVISED BY THE MARYLEBONE CLUB,

IN THE YEAR 1828,

OBSERVED BY THE WESTERN CRICKET CLUB OF GLASGOW,

INSTITUTED IN 1829.

THE BALL

1. MUST not weigh less than five Ounces and a half nor more than five Ounces and three quarters. At the beginning of each Innings either Party may call for a new Ball.

THE BAT

2. Must not exceed four Inches and one quarter in the widest part.

THE STUMPS

3. Must be twenty-seven Inches out of the Ground; the BAILS eight Inches in length; the Stumps of sufficient thickness to prevent the Ball from passing through.

THE BOWLING CREASE

4. Must be in a line with the Stumps, six Feet eight Inches in length; the Stumps in the Centre; with a RETURN CREASE at each end towards the Bowler at right angles.

THE POPPING CREASE

5. Must be four Feet from the Wicket, and parallel to it.

THE WICKETS

6. Must be pitched opposite to each other by the Umpires, at the distance of twenty-two Yards.

7. It shall not be lawful for either Party during a Match, without the consent of the other, to alter the Ground by rolling, watering, covering, mowing, or beating; This Rule is not meant to prevent the Striker from beating the Ground with his Bat near where he stands during the Innings, nor to prevent the Bowler from filling up holes with Sawdust, &c., when the Ground shall be wet.

8. After Rain the Wickets may be changed with the consent of both parties.

THE BOWLER

9. Shall deliver the Ball with one Foot behind the Bowling Crease, and within the Return Crease; and shall bowl four Balls before he change Wickets, which he shall be permitted to do but once in the same Innings.

10. The ball shall be bowled. If it be thrown or jerked, or if any part of the hand or arm be above the Elbow at the time of delivery, the Umpire shall call "No Ball"

11. He may order the Striker at his Wicket to stand on which side of it he pleases.

12. If the Bowler toss the Ball over the Striker's

Head, or bowl it so wide that it shall be out of distance to be played at, the Umpire (even although he attempt to hit it) shall adjudge one run to the parties receiving the Innings, either with or without an appeal from them; which shall be put down to the score of wide Balls, and such Ball shall not be reckoned as any of the four Balls.

13. If the Bowler bowl a "*No Ball,*" the Striker may play at it, and be allowed all the Runs he can get; and shall not be put out, except by running out.

14. In the event of a change of bowling, no more than two Balls shall be allowed in Practice.

15. The Bowler who takes the two Balls, shall be obliged to bowl four Balls.

THE STRIKER IS OUT

16. If the Bail be bowled off, or the Stump bowled out of the Ground.

17. Or, if the Ball, from a Stroke of the Bat, or hand, but not wrist, be held before it touch the Ground, although it be hugged to the body of the Catcher.

18. Or, if in striking, or at any other time while the Ball shall be in play, both his feet be over the Popping Crease, and his Wicket put down, except his Bat be grounded within it.

19. Or, if in striking at the Ball, he hit down his Wicket.

20. Or, if under pretence of running or otherwise, either of the Strikers prevent a Ball from being caught, the Striker of the Ball is out.

4

21. Or, if the Ball be struck, and he wilfully strike it again.

22. Or, if, in running, the Wicket be struck down by a throw, or by the hand or arm, (with ball in hand) before his Foot, Hand, or Bat be grounded over the Popping Crease. But, if the Bail be off, the Stump must be struck out of the ground.

23. Or, if any part of the Striker's Dress knock down the Wicket.

24. Or, if the Striker touch, or take up the Ball while in play, unless at the request of the other party.

25. Or, if, with any part of his person, he stop the Ball, which, in the opinion of the Umpire at the Bowler's Wicket, shall have been delivered in a straight line to the Striker's Wicket, and would have hit it.

26. If the Players have crossed each other, he that runs for the Wicket which is put down is out.

27. When a Ball shall be caught, no Run shall be reckoned.

28. When a Striker shall be run out, the Run which they were attempting shall not be reckoned.

29. If a lost Ball shall be called, the Striker shall be allowed six Runs; but, if more than six shall have been run before lost Ball shall have been called, then the Striker shall have all which have been run.

30. When the Ball has been in the Bowler's, or Wicket Keeper's Hands it is considered as no longer in play; and the Strikers need not keep within their

Ground till the Umpire has called "*Play;*" but, if the Player go out of his Ground with an intent to run before the Ball be delivered, the Bowler may put him out.

31. If the Striker be hurt, he may retire from his Wicket, and return to it at any time in that Innings.

32. If a Striker be hurt, some other person may be allowed to stand out for him, but not to go in.

33. No Substitute in the Field shall be allowed to bowl, keep Wicket, stand at the Point, or middle Wicket, or stop behind to a fast Bowler, unless with the consent of the adverse Party. The Umpires shall enforce this Law.

34. If any Person stop the Ball with his Hat the Ball shall be considered dead, and the opposite party shall add five Runs to their score; if any be run, they shall have five in all.

35. If the Ball be struck the Striker may guard his Wicket either with his Bat or his Body.

THE WICKET KEEPER

36. Shall stand at a reasonable Distance behind the Wicket, and shall not move till the Ball be out of the Bowler's Hand, and shall not by any noise incommode the Striker; and if any part of his Person be over or before the Wicket, although the Ball hit it, the Striker shall not be out.

THE UMPIRES

37. Are sole Judges of fair and unfair Play; and all Disputes shall be determined by them, each at his own Wicket: but in case of a Catch which the Um-

6

pire at the Wicket bowled from cannot see sufficiently to decide upon he may apply to the other Umpire whose opinion is conclusive.

38. The Umpires in all Matches shall pitch fair Wickets, and the Parties shall toss for the Choice of Innings.

39. They shall allow two Minutes for each man to come in, and fifteen Minutes between each Innings. When the Umpires shall call "*Play,*" the Party refusing to play, shall lose the Match.

40. They are not to order a Player out, unless appealed to by the Adversaries.

41. But, if the Bowler's Foot be not behind the Bowling Crease, within the Return Crease, when he shall deliver the Ball, they must, unasked call "*No Ball.*"

42. If the Striker run a short Run, the Umpire must call "*One Short.*"

43. The Umpires are not to be changed during the Match, but by the consent of both Parties.

LAWS FOR SINGLE WICKET.

1. When there shall be less than five Players on a side, Bounds shall be placed twenty-two yards each in a line from the Off, and Leg Stump.

2. The Ball must be hit before the Bounds to entitle the Striker to a Run; which Run cannot be obtained unless he touch the Bowling Stump or Crease

in a line with it with his Bat, or some part of his Person; or go beyond them; returning to the Popping Crease, as at double Wicket, according to the 22nd Law.

3. When the Striker shall hit the Ball, one of his Feet must be on the Ground, and behind the Popping Crease, otherwise the Umpire shall call "*No Hit.*"

4. When there shall be less than five Players on a side, neither Byes nor Overthrows shall be allowed; nor shall the Striker be caught out behind Wicket, nor stumped out.

5. The Field's Man must return the Ball so that it shall cross the Play between the Wicket and the Bowling Stump, or between the Bowling Stump and the Bounds; the Striker may run till the Ball shall be so returned.

6. After the Striker shall have made one Run, if he start again, he must touch the Bowling Stump, and turn before the Ball shall cross the play to entitle him to another.

7. The Striker shall be entitled to three Runs for lost Ball, and the same number for Ball stopped with Hat; with reference to the 29th and 34th Laws at double Wicket.

8. When there shall be more than four Players on a side, there shall be no Bounds. All Hits, Byes, and Overthrows, shall then be allowed.

9. The Bowler is subject to the same Laws as at double Wicket.

10. Not more than one Minute shall be allowed between each Ball.

8

BETS.

If the Runs of one Player be laid against those of another, the Bets depend on the first Innings, unless otherwise specified.

If the Bets be made upon both Innings, and one Party beat the other in one Innings, the Runs in the first Innings shall determine the Bet.

But if the other Party go in a second Time, then the Bet must be determined by the number on the Score.

Members.

James Steven, *President.*
Charles Campbell, *Treasurer.*
David Murray, *Secretary.*
John Wright.
5. D. J. Penney.
Andrew Muir.
Robert Maxwell.
William Mann.
John Warden.
10. Thomas Ovington.
Robert M'Callum.

} *Committee or Directors.*

John Edwards.
John Steven.
Andrew Campbell.
15. James M'Lachlane.
Thomas Stevenson, jun.
R. C. Wilson.
John Mair.
Robert Crombie.
20. William Glen.
Mathew Taylor.
Andrew Muir.
William Muir.
R. M. Smith.
25. John C. Todd.
Robert Adam.
James Farley.
William Mather.

John Mather.
30. ——— Jephson.
Robert Thomson.
Andrew Dunlop.
Alexander Buchanan.
James Warden.
35. John Thomson.
Robert Govane.
James Henderson.
William Smith.
William Hussey, jun.
40. Edward S. Busby.
Gilbert Bogle.
Henry Sherriff.
William Merry.
Kenneth Morison.
45. George Wicks.
T. M. M. Weller.
——— Hutchison.
John Galloway.
George Duncan.
50. Henry Hussey.
Walter Campbell.
Neil Bannatyne.
Henry Littledale.
Thomas M'Kay.
55. Robert Patterson.
John White.
Alexander Mather.
Walter Forrester.

James Watson.
60. William Mills.
Charles Gray.
William Sloan.
Robert D. Hamilton.
John Jaffray.
65. Andrew M'Feat.
John Graham.
William Bentley, jun.
J. Gibb.
Alexander Wilson.
70. ——— Stein.
Robert Ewing.
Alexander Taylor.
James Taylor.
John Wilson.
75. Henry Wilkinson.
Edward D. Walker.
Charles Scott.
John Moody.
Walter Jamieson.
80. Walter Lees.
William Smith.
James Craig.
Alexander Grant.
John Walker.
85. Alexander Dyce.
William Lumsden.
Thomas King.
——— M'George.
——— Elliot.

Cricket - Perceptions.

Cricket - It's a word that evokes images of sunny afternoons, chaps in white flannels, village greens, buxom ladies with kindly rose-cheeked faces serving cucumber sandwiches and cups of tea, of order and politeness, of quaint and gentile, almost twee behaviour, and to the world, something that is regarded as being instantly recognisable as quintessentially English.

To many others, it falsely triggers reactions of what they feel is an anathema to them. Empire, colonialism, conquest, subjugation of the natives, the raping of resources for personal profit, Queen and country, upper class elitism, old-boy networks, imposed structure and order upon the masses by a privileged minority and the delivery of a clinical form of assertive democracy.

To most Scots, cricket is just simply a game perceived to be played by an elite with middle and upper class pretensions and is unfortunately treated with complete and utter contempt and disdain by the majority of its denizens.

The reality, especially in a west of Scotland perspective, is completely the opposite and it is a sport that triggered the globalisation of another sport, namely football, and football's success as the "peoples game" can be traced right back to the determination of a handful of Glasgow area cricket clubs, their founders and patrons, and most importantly, their members, all of whom were mainly from humble beginnings and working class backgrounds, and who have never received the thanks and gratitude that they so richly deserve from the generations that have followed.

Cricket was, and still is, Scotland's national team sport. Its importance has been lost and its history has been trampled underfoot and discarded as meaningless as other sports and pastimes have emerged.

"No one, except a close observer, can believe the earnestness and enthusiasm imparted into the game by the formation of young clubs, but there is one danger which should be avoided. There is such a thing as overdoing; and, depend upon it, if this is continued, the game will suffer. To those who love and appreciate everything in season, the advice I am about to impart will be doubly significant.

Football is a winter game, and while it may be all right to practice in spring and autumn, the line is bound to be drawn somewhere, and why attempt to force it down the throats of cricketers, athletes, yachtsmen, and even lawn-tennis players, in the heart of summer? It must not be forgotten that some of our best and most influential football clubs have also cricket clubs and kindred summer recreations attached, and, in the interests of football, these should be encouraged; and to this end I am confident my remarks will be treated with some respect.

I am also sure that no one who has taken a deep interest in the game from its comparative infancy, but can look back with extreme pleasure on its development, and even go the length of registering a vow that he will do his utmost to make and uphold it as an honest and manly game, despite isolated assumptions by a few traducers who question such earnestness, and I will endeavour to point them out, and draw comparisons."

David Drummond Bone

Scottish Football Reminiscences and Sketches 1890.

As the Willow Vanishes – Glasgow's Forgotten Legacy

"As The Willow Vanishes" will hopefully change these perceptions by explaining Glasgow's forgotten legacy to the world - the importance of what its cricket introduced, its impact on the socio political, economic and historical fabric of a United Kingdom and beyond, while detailing the legacies that it created and exploring the cultural impact that it has had on local communities and populations.

It is my personal opinion of course, but an increasingly cynical and jaundiced society has resulted in most adopting a parochial and selfish attitude to life, whether it be in work, recreation or socially. The paramount importance appears to be of an individual's welfare and self importance while completely disregarding those around them, who and how they interact with them and the impact that such behaviours have. It is important to take stock of the attributes that define you as a person, because the skill sets you acquire throughout your life are like the qualities you require for cricket.

Cricket is a team game where your fortunes are determined by those you play with and how you play with them. Some team-mates are good, some team-mates are bad, some are selfish, some are show-offs, some try their hardest and others are just simply ordinary enthusiasts. But collectively, it is a combined resolve to achieve something together that is not only rewarding, but beneficial to all involved. The analogy does apply when you assess your life, and the meaningful milestones that you pass on its journey through the years are the reflective considerations of what success you have achieved or contributed to.

What component of the team are you?

Cultural Impact

Cricket's impact on popular culture around the world is clear to see. Its influence on the English language is evident with phrases such as "that's not cricket" referring to something that is unfair, "had a good innings" usually in relation to someone who has enjoyed a long life, "sticky wicket" normally coined when someone is faced with a degree of difficulty, "stumped" when bewildered or stuck with a particular task, and "bowled over" when someone has been completely astounded at a situation or circumstance before them.

There are so many of them in everyday conversation, their origin has become lost on the users. The term "Bradmanesque" derived from the surname of the ultimate Australian sporting hero, Sir Donald Bradman, has become a generic term for outstanding excellence, both within cricket and in the wider world.

Cricket is a unique game, where in addition to its laws, the players have to abide by the "Spirit of the Game". This spirit refers to a standard of sportsmanship that has historically been considered so high that the phrase "it's just not cricket" was coined in the 19th century to describe unfair or underhanded behaviour in any walk of life. A sport whose ethics have essentially become a template for everyone to appreciate in everyday life by demonstrating fairness, compassion, empathy, abiding by laws, rules and regulations, respect for others, doing things correctly and inside the expected parameters of what is acceptable.

Its ethics now seem to be sadly missing elsewhere, whether it is in other sports, business or life.

An Interpretation of One's Psyche

As a child, I was fortunate that my father and my elder siblings all played, or had an interest, in cricket. My father had played and been involved in the sport all his life and was insistent that his children would follow suit. He had grown up in the Shawlands area of Glasgow, had attended the local Shawlands Academy and for him to play cricket for the school, he had to become a member of Poloc Cricket Club, which he joined and played for before and after the Second World War. His other sporting love had been football and he was honoured to have been a youth player at Queen's Park until his football career was cut short when he contracted typhoid at the age of 18. All through my formative years, I spent summer weekends at cricket grounds throughout the west of Scotland. Although he was no longer playing, my father liked to watch a number of games every weekend and I was dragged along, with bat and ball, and told to go away and find something to do.

Test matches against similar children of various clubs ensued repeatedly over the summers of the 1970s, and friendships and associations were made to last a lifetime. It wasn't only the playing of cricket that occurred, but the exploration of the cricket grounds and their environs that followed, interspersed with mischief, incidents, scrapes and injuries that more often than not resulted in me getting an extremely stern talking to for spoiling my father's watching of cricket.

I didn't understand at the time why my father would get so upset when his weekend's spectating was interrupted with taking me to the local accident and emergency unit for whatever latest injury to be attended to, and I couldn't really comprehend why his ire at my behaviour was so intense, but as I got older, I slowly began to appreciate what my father, in his awkward manner, was attempting to instill in me. An appreciation of the game for what it is and also the greater aspects associated with the game.

It wasn't just simply about participation and involvement in and around a particular sport, it was also about preparing you for life, how you dealt with its successes and disappointments, its tragedies, working with others, camaraderie and friendships, recognising and understanding the character traits and the frailties attached to those you met, experiencing Machiavellian machinations and politics and how you reacted to them, but most importantly, instilling within you a sense of altruism.

The Answers for the Future Lie In The Past

As a cricketer, I have enjoyed playing the sport all over Scotland, against various teams, clubs and selects, and while I have been fortunate to have experienced success along the way, I have also been privileged to have played on over three hundred grounds in Scotland alone. Playing on that amount of grounds has given me a greater appreciation of what others have to do to get a game of cricket organised, let alone played. I have met many people, some famous and most that are not, but meeting them and sharing the associations that only cricket provides, has made me feel grateful for their time, whether it be merely a fleeting acquaintance or a lengthy friendship or acknowledgement.

Up to the age of about 30, my provision of cricket had been structured, ordered and following a template of annual repetitiveness that conditioned you to a familiarity of expectation that provoked apathy, even contempt, whenever you encountered cricket that existed outside your normal sphere of contact. My competitive cricket involved a "closed shop" of the same ten clubs with occasional sorties around the country in national cups and friendlies. This "closed shop" was called the Western Union and its clubs were Ayr, Clydesdale, Drumpellier, Ferguslie, Greenock, Kelburne, Kilmarnock, Poloc, Uddingston and West of Scotland.

I sought fresh challenges for personal reasons and I moved outside of the bubble of isolation of the Western Union. I was unaware of what others enjoyed and appreciated, but having shaken off the comfort blanket that had surrounded me from childhood, I became fascinated with what I was about to encounter. The meeting of new faces, new grounds, new opinions, different outlooks and practices, new experiences and a whole host of characters changed my interpretation and understanding of cricket in Scotland forever, but bizarrely, this voyage took me back to the point of origin, the Western Union, and the start of a five year quest to find answers to the many questions that I had gathered over the years and a mission to prove or disprove a personal theory – "Big House" cricket.

It was when I started to research the history of the beginnings of cricket in the west of Scotland that I began to discover all sorts of interesting stories, bizarre tales and exploits that seemed to be just beyond the realms of truth. There were hints of how cricket became popular at first and that it appeared that the landed gentry simply favoured private matches amongst themselves, arranged them and enjoyed the profits of wagers placed. I needed to investigate this. The burning questions were how did cricket suddenly appear in the west of Scotland with a structure of organised clubs that led to developed leagues and competitions, but also why did it seem to have had such an influence on other sports and past-times?

To understand the fervour of the many that I had met over the years, I had to appreciate first of all that the playing of the game itself, was, in fact, actually a minor matter, and that it was everything else attached to co-ordinating and arranging of the game that were the major factors. From preparing the pitch to ensuring the teams were available to having enough food and provisions for teas to having scorers and umpires. It was the expectancy of the game and all that is around it that is actually more important than the match. The match happens and someone wins and someone loses, but the match is also an event. It is a form of social gathering that features grace, etiquette, manners and interaction while incorporating a sporting clash to determine victors and bragging rights.

To find these answers, one has to have some form of rudimentary appreciation and understanding of the concept, and for that to happen, the past would have to be researched.

"Big House" cricket seemed to be a particular favourite in the early days of west cricket and it appeared, at first, that it was a pastime where the wealthy reveled in participating in matches had been arranged by whomever. It was of no importance as to who was actually playing for whatever team, but what was of importance was that a game was being played and that an occasion had been completed that was of benefit to all concerned, on and off the field of play.

This concept of "Big House" cricket is actually very difficult to explain but it can be simplified down to a relatively basic equation.

venue + resources + players = game + networks + opportunity

If you have a venue, you can gather family, friends, associates, employees and business contacts together to mix with each other and enjoy participation in all that surrounds a game of cricket, and with creating a game and generating an atmosphere of involvement that would not normally exist, let alone operate, you inculcate introductions, dialogues and interactions that generate networks to be built and lay the foundations for the establishment of opportunity, whether it be for personal or professional gain.

To fully appreciate what the concept of "Big House" cricket may be responsible for bringing about, you have to know the back story to its creation which begins in Alloway, famous for Rabbie Burns, witches and the legend of Tam O'Shanter.

A James Baird, who lived in Cambusdoon House on the Cambusdoon Estate just outside of Ayr, was one such chap who loved "big house" cricket. A member of the Lanarkshire family of iron-masters who had made their fortune in the industrial revolution, James purchased the 20,000 acre site, changed its name from Greenfield to Cambusdoon and had Cambusdoon House built in 1853.

Cricket matches were played on the front lawn and eventually, in 1859, much to the demand for the creation of a cricket club by the local population, Ayr Cricket Club was founded. Other clubs began to spring up in the local area and by the year 1870, Ayr was home to three clubs.

By 1876, other cricket clubs had appeared in Ayr and the sport appeared to be gaining popularity in the community.

CRICKET CLUBS.

AYR CLUB.

Patron, The Most Noble the Marquis of Bute.
President, J. S. M'Iwraith
Captain, G. B. Phillips. *Vice-Captain*, W. Blane
Sec. and Treas. Q. Blane

EGLINTON CLUB.

Patron, The Right Hon. the Earl of Eglinton and Winton
President, James B. Paton
Captain, James Thomson *Vice-Captain*, John Paterson
Secretary, A. B. Young *Treasurer*, William Wilson

THISTLE CLUB.

Patron, Col. Alexander of Ballochmyle
President, A. D. Wilson
Captain, Alexander Reid *Vice-Captain*, John Govan.
Sec. and Treas., John Hunter

ST. ANDREW'S CLUB.

Patron—Henry Houldsworth, Esq., Carrick House.
President—J. B. Paton, Esq.
Captain—R. K. Adams. Vice-Captain—J. Jamieson.
Treasurer—W. Highet, jr.
Secy.—J. L. Hutcheon, 49 Newmarket Street.

The Ayr club itself was the senior of all the local sides and by 1888 seemed set in the grounds of Falkland Park.

AYR CRICKET CLUB.
Ground - Falkland Park, Prestwick Road.
Patron The Earl of Stair, K.T.
Hon. President—R. F. F. Campbell, Esq., M.P.
President J. B. Paton, Esq.
Vice-Presidents—Dr Naismith and R. M. Davidson, Esq.
Captain—Mr Andrew Mark. Vice-Captain—Mr J. T. Goudie.
Second XI. Captain—Mr J. Cochrane.
Secretary and Treasurer—Mr J. M'Call, 38 Sandgate Street.
Committee—Messrs Hunter, Phillips, Cooper, Willet, Macintosh, and Cochrane.
Match Committee—Messrs Mark, M'Call, and Cochrane.

But by 1890, Ayr Cricket Club had moved across the road to a new ground in Northfield Park.

AYR CRICKET CLUB.
Ground—Northfield Park, Prestwick Road.
Patron—The Earl of Stair, K.T.
Hon. President—J. Douglas Baird, Esq.
Hon. Vice-Presidents—D. A. S. Cuninghame, Esq., W. Baird, Esq
President—J. B. Paton, Esq.
Vice-Presidents—R. M. Davidson, Esq., Dr Naismith.
Chairman of Committees—Mr J. K. Hunter.
Hon. Secretary and Treasurer—Mr T. D. Wallace, 12 John St.
Match Secretary—Mr James M'Call, 38 Sandgate Street.
2nd Eleven Captain—Mr M. Arthur.
Committee—Messrs Philips, Mark, Wallace, Greig, Arthur, J. M. Jamieson, Cochran, Willet, and M'Call.
Match Committee—Messrs Mark, Willet, Cooper, M'Call, Arthur, and Greig.

As the Nineteenth Century came to a close, Ayr Cricket Club moved ground again to Dam Park and remained there for thirty-five seasons.

AYR CRICKET CLUB (INSTITUTED 1859.)
Ground—Dampark.
Patron—The Marquis of Bute, K.T.
Hon. President—Charles L. Orr-Ewing, Esq., M.P.
Hon. Vice-Presidents—D. A. Smith Cunningham, Esq.; J. M. Houldsworth, Esq.; Wm. Baird, Esq.; R. M. Pollok, Esq.; W. H. Dunlop, Esq.; and J. A. Campbell, Esq.
President—Dr Naismith.
Vice-Presidents—R. M. Davidson, Esq., & Jas. Arthur, Esq.
Secretary—W. J. Dewar, 8 Millar Road.
Hon. Treasurer—W. Robertson, 11 Hawkhill.
Match Secretaries—James M'Call, 38 Sandgate Street, and W. J. Dewar, 8 Millar Road.
Captain—P. Goudie. Vice-Captain—W. Robertson.
Second Eleven Captain—J. K. Hunter.
Vice-Captain—J. M'Feat.
Committee—Messrs P. Goudie, W. Robertson, J. T. Goudie, J. M'Call, J. K. Hunter, J. W. Ralston, C. S. Gray, J. M. Jamieson, J. Hayman, F. Ferguson, and W. J. Dewar.
Match Committee—The Captains and Vice-Captains of both Elevens, and the Match Secretaries.

AYR VICTORIA CRICKET CLUB.
Ground—Racecourse.
Patrons—C. L. Orr-Ewing, Esq., M.P.; J. H. Houldsworth, Esq.; R. M. Pollok, Esq.; J. B. Fergusson, Esq.; and Provost Templeton.
Hon. President—John Cameron.
President—James Lochhead.
Vice-President—J. Forbes Thomson.
Captain—J. Steele. Vice-Captain—A. D. Thomson.
Secretary and Treasurer—J. M'Cartney, Seafield Lodge.

There were still other clubs in Ayr at the time, and one of which was Ayr Victoria who operated out of the Racecourse.

AYR VICTORIA CRICKET CLUB.
Ground—Racecourse.
Patrons—C. L. Orr-Ewing, Esq., M.P.; J. H. Houldsworth, Esq.; R. M. Pollok, Esq.; J. B. Fergusson, Esq.; and Provost Templeton.
Hon. President—John Cameron.
President—James Lochhead.
Vice-President—J. Forbes Thomson.
Captain—J. Steele. Vice-Captain—A. D. Thomson.
Secretary and Treasurer—J. M'Cartney, Seafield Lodge.

Both of these cricket clubs seemed to enjoy the support of the local MP, Charles L. Orr-Ewing, a member of an extended family that had associations at a number of other clubs, and the Messrs Houldsworth, successful cotton spinners, machinery makers, iron founders and iron masters in Lanarkshire and in Ayrshire, who were also patrons of the West of Scotland Cricket Club in Glasgow.

Ayr Cricket Club moved from their Dam Park venue to the Cambusdoon Estate and their famous Cambusdoon ground in 1935, where it remained their home for 60 years until it was sold for housing in 1995.

James Baird's original Cambusdoon House, which by then was nothing more than a ruin, had been converted into a boys' preparatory school in the late 1920s, and the rest of the estate surrounding the cricket ground was developed for housing in the late 1930s.

The former England cricket captain, Mike Denness, grew up in one of the houses on Shanter Way, which adjoined the cricket ground.

In 1996, Ayr Cricket Club moved across the road to Robertson's Field and a bespoke facility, and changed the name of the ground to New Cambusdoon.

The Last Game At Cambusdoon

Of all the Scottish grounds, Cambusdoon is probably my favourite for many reasons. It has always been a happy hunting ground for me as a bowler, but I always associate it as a place where I have always felt comfortable and welcomed. This association passes back through my family to my parents and the late 1940s, early 1950s. My mother, Dagny, was a Danish national who met my father during World War II.

My mother had worked in Berlin from early in 1938 right to the outbreak of the war when she escaped into Denmark, embarked on the last ship out of Copenhagen and made her way back home to the Faroe Islands.

English was her fourth language after Faroese, her native tongue, Danish and then German. She had only spoken English while she had been in Berlin and consequently spoke with a German accent. In the aftermath of the war, on her arrival in Scotland, she was treated with suspicion and contempt by most due to her thick German accent.

However, as she travelled with my father to his various matches on his return to cricket for Poloc after his war service, Ayr Cricket Club was the one club that she always said made her to feel the most welcome and it was a club where she made many friendships over the subsequent years.

In the latter years of her life, after the death of my father, Dagny moved down to Ayr and lived a short distance from the cricket ground. In early September 1996, when I was playing for GHK Cricket Club, along with my brother Eric, we were both fortunate to play against Ayr in what happened to be the last ever game of cricket to take place at the Cambusdoon ground.

It turned out to be a super match, in which, both sides played the game in a splendidly sporting atmosphere befitting the occasion, and where Ayr attempted to chase down a reasonable total on a gloriously sunny Sunday afternoon.

Although now in failing health, Dagny was most insistent on coming along to Cambusoon to watch the game, and Eric and I acceded to her demands. It was the last cricket match that she ever attended.

Wickets fell and at 9 down with six runs required off the last over for victory, the then Ayr Chairman, Norman Simpson, was facing the final ever over to be bowled at Cambusdoon. Norman clipped the first ball off his legs and scampered a single. Five required. The other batsman misses balls 2, 3 and 4 and then sclaffs a horrible hoik to midwicket for a single leaving Norman Simpson to face the last ever ball. The years rolled back and Norman majestically stroked the ball through extra cover and we all watched the ball rebound off the pavilion's boundary picket fence.

It was with both pride and sadness that Norman accepted from GHK the gift of the match ball as a trophy to mark what was a historic day in the annals of Ayr Cricket Club – a perfect end to the playing of cricket at Cambusdoon with Norman hitting the final ever runs to be scored, fittingly a winning boundary, on the ground.

The following season in 1997, GHK drew Ayr in the quarter-final of the Scottish Cup at New Cambusdoon. Ayr had been undefeated at their new ground and this was going to be a hard game. Again it was a gloriously sunny Sunday afternoon and a large crowd was in attendance to watch the game. Ayr 197ao played GHK 198 for 6 and again another little piece of history had unfolded. Not only had GHK been the first side to beat Ayr at their new ground but they had progressed to their first ever Scottish Cup semi-final. Norman Simpson walked into an obviously jubilant GHK dressing room with a jug of lager for the players. He placed the jug of lager down on a seat, congratulated GHK on their win, reached into his trouser pocket and retrieved the match ball and "presented" it to GHK and wished them all the best for the rest of the season. Reciprocity at its sporting best.

A few years later, my mother passed away and her funeral wake was held in the clubhouse at New Cambusdoon. It seemed an appropriate gesture for the remembrance and farewell of her life to be held at a place where Dagny was always at her happiest.

The Coatbridge Connector

The changes made by the success of the industrialisation of the west coast of Scotland were beginning to leave their marks, as the landscape of a once agricultural society altered.

Two other west clubs that can hold their existences aloft as a result of "Big House" cricket are Drumpellier and West of Scotland Cricket Clubs. Both clubs have a Colonel David Carrick Robert Carrick Buchanan to thank for their founding.

Colonel David Carrick Robert Carrick Buchanan of Drumpellier and Mount Vernon, was born in 1825 and was married to a Frances Lefroy, granddaughter of the former Chief Justice of Ireland. He was a Colonel of the 2nd Royal Lanark Militia, and was also Master of the Lanark and Renfrew Hunt. He also had estates such as Finlayston in Renfrewshire, the ancient seat of the Glencairns, and Carradale and Torrisdale in Cantyre.

The family wealth had been initially made in the Americas and through the tobacco trade, but diversification into other areas such as land management and urban development maintained and continued the riches.

Colonel David Carrick Robert Carrick Buchanan truly loved the sport of cricket. As a perfect example of the concept of "Big House" cricket, he just simply formed his own side, initially made up of his friends and servants, and they played in the picturesque setting of the grounds of his main home, Drumpellier House.

By 1850, cricket had become established in the surrounding villages, with many teams filled by workers who had travelled from Lancashire to Lanarkshire seeking employment as the industrial revolution expanded.

The influence of Colonel David Carrick Robert Carrick Buchanan upon the establishment of cricket in the greater Glasgow area was certainly profound, but I was completely unaware of and totally unprepared for what I was going to discover, and that my basic equation for "Big House" cricket,

venue + resources + players = game + networks + opportunity

was of a far greater significance than I had ever anticipated.

On searching the history, Colonel David Carrick Robert Carrick Buchanan is revealed as a man of great stature and influence, but in doing so, one also learns of his great patronage of Scottish cricket and the influential support he exerted on the establishment of a number of clubs. His pride and joy was his own club Drumpellier, which lay at the bottom of his front lawn.

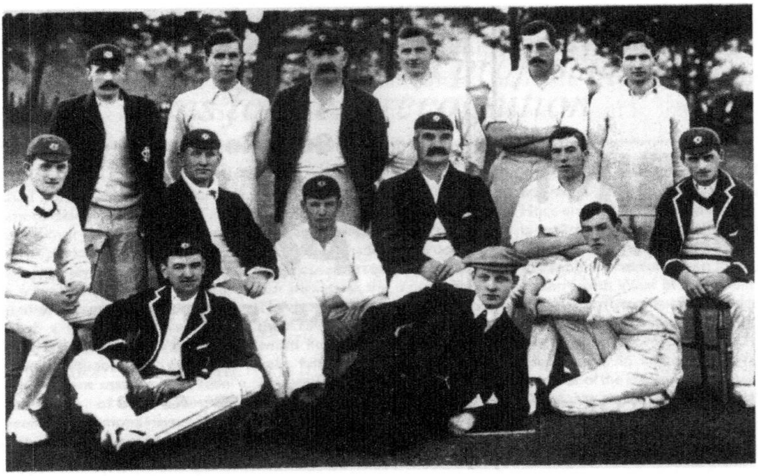

Drumpellier's establishment as a dominant cricket club was achieved by the Colonel's engagement of a professional cricketer called John Sands. Sands, originally from Sussex, had eked out a career at Edinburgh Academy, Clydesdale and West of Scotland, and at the latter of the three, his expertise had been essential in the design and landscaping of the ground at Hamilton Crescent.

Sands' arrival at Drumpellier in 1864 heralded the beginning of 25 years continuous service as the club's professionally employed cricketer and where his coaching skills transformed the club into an academy of cricket.

Such was the success of what was being developed that an invitation was sent to Dr. W.G. Grace to bring the United South of England eleven to play a three day match against the twenty-two of Drumpellier. The good Doctor did and Drumpellier secured a famous victory. In that same year, Drumpellier lost only one of their matches and Johnny Sands' work ensured that Drumpellier became established as one of the great cricket clubs in Scotland.

Sands, John, cricket emporium, Langloan

SANDS, John, cricket depot, 31 Langloan, Coatbridge.

Colonel David Carrick Robert Carrick Buchanan's contribution to cricket is not really appreciated, but his devotion to the local community of Coatbridge was immense. Such was the respect and reverence for the man, that in his final years, when he would wander down from the big house to watch the cricket at the foot of his garden, he would take the straightest route possible to get to the pavilion.

The path would be across the square and the field of play, a course of action that would normally bring strong reactions from the players and spectators towards the trespasser, but this was the man from the "Big House" and play stopped to allow him to pass.

After finding out more about the man's involvement in the shaping of Glasgow as a city, not only was he entitled to the acknowledgement, he fully deserved it.

Drumpellier Cricket Club—Col. D. C. R. C. Buchanan, C.B. president & captain; Captain G. F. R. Colt, vice-president; David Crichton, sec. & treasurer

Buchanan Street in Glasgow was named after the Buchanan family whose various tobacco interests brought great wealth to the city. The land around the north and northeast of Buchanan Street was formerly home to Buchanan Street railway station and was originally owned by the Caledonian Railway. Not a bad effort in respect of the family's influence.

Colonel David Carrick Robert Carrick Buchanan's association with West of Scotland Cricket Club is probably the better known of his various patronages. His involvement with the club began in 1862, the year the club was founded, when he was present at a meeting that was held in the Clarence Hotel in George Square in Glasgow.

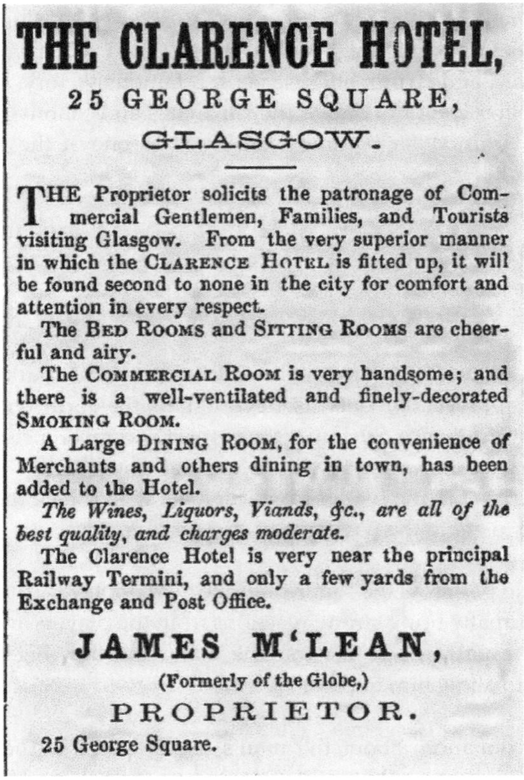
THE CLARENCE HOTEL,
25 GEORGE SQUARE,
GLASGOW.
THE Proprietor solicits the patronage of Commercial Gentlemen, Families, and Tourists visiting Glasgow. From the very superior manner in which the Clarence Hotel is fitted up, it will be found second to none in the city for comfort and attention in every respect.
The Bed Rooms and Sitting Rooms are cheerful and airy.
The Commercial Room is very handsome; and there is a well-ventilated and finely-decorated Smoking Room.
A Large Dining Room, for the convenience of Merchants and others dining in town, has been added to the Hotel.
The Wines, Liquors, Viands, &c., are all of the best quality, and charges moderate.
The Clarence Hotel is very near the principal Railway Termini, and only a few yards from the Exchange and Post Office.
JAMES M'LEAN,
(Formerly of the Globe,)
PROPRIETOR.
25 George Square.

The meeting had been arranged between a number of local businessmen and the representatives and players of Clutha Cricket Club. Clutha Cricket Club who had formed previously in 1858, were at the time of this meeting, the then users of the playing field that would become Hamilton Crescent, the home of the new West of Scotland Cricket Club.

Colonel David Carrick Robert Carrick Buchanan became the first President of the new West of Scotland Cricket Club and remained so until his death in 1903.

The name of the club, West of Scotland Cricket Club, was the idea of one of the businessmen present at the original meeting, a John McNeill. John McNeill was perhaps a man ahead of his time in that he had a number of plans for the future and further development of the new West of Scotland Cricket Club.

McNeill's vision was to create a Scottish equivalent of the MCC and also make West of Scotland Cricket Club the powerhouse and centre of excellence for the sport in Scotland. All-England Elevens became frequent visitors to Hamilton Crescent culminating in Dr. W.G. Grace bringing a team in 1891. Many other such fixtures were arranged, which included the first ever visit of an Australian team to Scotland in 1878.

West of Scotland Cricket Club had established itself as a cricket club of considerable stature and Hamilton Crescent had become, not only the Glasgow venue for various prestigious cricket matches, but as the ground for the playing of many important games of rugby and football that established those respective sports.

WEST OF SCOTLAND CRICKET CLUB.

GROUND—HAMILTON CRESCENT, PARTICK.

Sir Michael Shaw Stewart, Bart., Sir Robert Milliken Napier, Bart., Sir Archibald Islay Campbell, Bart., the Hon. George F. Boyle, Robert Dalglish, M.P., William Graham, M.P., W. S. Stirling Crawford, the Messrs. Houldsworth, patrons; Colonel D. C. R. Carrick Buchanan, Drumpellier, president; W. C. Paterson, Ashville, Partick, vice-president.

LIST OF MATCHES.—April 18, at Partick, W. S. C. C, v. Officers of 21st Regt.—Opening match and promenade. May 18, 19, at Partick, v. Grange. May 24, 25, 26, at Partick, v. All England Eleven. June 2, at Perth, v. Perthshire. June 6, 7, at Partick, v. North of Ireland. June 9, at Partick, v. Dalkeith. June 16, at Partick, v. Officers of 21st Regiment—return match. June 23, at Stirling, v. Stirlingshire. June 30, at Partick, v. Drumpellier. July 6, 7, at Edinburgh, v. Grange—return match. July 13, 14, at Belfast, v. North of Ireland—return match. July 14, at Partick, v. Merchiston Castle, with professional. July 21, at Partick, v. Stirlingshire—return match. July 28, at Partick, v. Perthshire. August 4, at Drumpellier, v. Drumpellier. August 8, 9, at Partick, v. Free Forresters. August 25, at Dalkeith, v. Dalkeith—return match. Sept. 22, at Partick, v. Closing Match and Promenade.

Matches are also in course of arrangement with the gentlemen of Ireland, borough of Tynemouth, Northumberland, Kelso, and various other clubs.

John M'Neill, James Lilburn, William Scott Paterson, John Binning, Daniel Duff, A. Hope Pattison, directors; John Gilfillan, Clyde View, Partick, hon. secretary; John M'Neill, G. E. Macvicar, John Gilfillan, joint-treasurers; William L. Baird, 55 Moray Place, Glasgow, match committee and Partick club secretary.

Subscriptions payable to John M'Neill, 20 Hope Street, Glasgow, or to any of the joint-treasurers on the ground only.

The photograph is of a group of gentlemen suitably attired to represent Glasgow in the annual inter-city cricket match against Edinburgh in 1873. The match, which was played at the West of Scotland Cricket Cub ground at Hamilton Crescent, Partick, was drawn.

1873

At one time, the inter-city match was played each year from 1872 until 1894 and was regarded as one of the highlights of the Scottish cricket season. A good crowd was assured, which raised revenue to help develop the sport. Over the years, honours were fairly even between the teams, but disputes over the introduction of professionalism finally killed off the fixture.

West of Scotland Cricket Club built an Indoor Cricket School behind the clubhouse in 1957. It was the first type of such facility to be built in Scotland and provided access to training all the year round. In 2011/2012, West of Scotland Cricket Club refurbished the facility as part of their 150th anniversary celebrations and also commenced large groundwork re-developments on the playing area to return the club back to being a venue for important fixtures.

My adult participation in cricket is as a direct result of the Indoor School. In November 1976, I was knocked down by a motor vehicle and sustained serious head and leg injuries. I underwent a number of operations and had fairly lengthy stays in hospital which resulted in a loss of sport and exercise. The injuries to my left leg were so serious that they would remain as open wounds for four years before finally healing.

I spent many hours of recuperation within the Indoor School receiving specialist coaching from Tom Atkinson, the club professional, and Len Issott, the club groundsman. Atkinson was from Nottinghamshire and Issott was from Yorkshire and both gentlemen were time-served cricket professionals. They understood the game inside out and were also experienced cricket groundsmen and their skills, knowledge and expertise were evident to see deployed at West of Scotland Cricket Club. Both men had an enthusiasm for the sport that is now rarely encountered and their commitment to help and assist me recover from serious injury has never been forgotten. It is only now in middle-age that I actually truly comprehend how much of their influence formed and shaped my appreciation of the game, and I am, and always will be, eternally grateful to both these men.

In 2012, West of Scotland Cricket Club appointed John Blain as the club coach. A successful international and professional county cricketer, his appointment, together with the various ongoing refurbishment and re-development ventures at Hamilton Crescent, are indications of a club looking at itself, its traditions and its past history and then drawing from them to re-assert itself back at the top of the game as a leading and important club in the 21st Century.

1890

2012

A Changing Estate

A third example of "Big House" cricket in the west was Poloc Cricket Club, founded in 1878, and who began life at the Pollokshaws Race Course and then moved to their Shawholm ground within the Pollok Estate in 1880. The Pollok Estate and much of the surrounding land on the south side of Glasgow belonged to Sir John Stirling Maxwell, the 10th Baronet, and in 1888 he afforded Poloc Cricket Club full tenancy of Shawholm. Sir John Stirling Maxwell's influence with Poloc Cricket Club continued until his death in 1956.

Poloc's ground of Shawholm is located at the beginning of the long avenue that leads to Pollok House. The clubhouse originally belonged to the Pollokshields Athletic Club that lay in another part of the estate, and after the athletics club had folded, the clubhouse was simply placed on rollers and moved through the estate and placed where it currently stands. A perfect example of Victorian ingenuity that appears to have been replicated a few years later at the neighbouring Titwood ground when its clubhouse was moved from across its policies.

Poloc Cricket Club became a focal point in the local community and in 1889, a six-hole golf course was built around the perimeter of the ground. The golf course is still used to this day and is the only 6-hole course with Royal & Ancient accreditation with regular medals and competitions throughout the winter months.

Other sports followed at the ground, such as bowls, tennis, putting and archery and in 1908, the Pollokshaws Working Lads Club formed a football team and drew players from amongst the ranks of cricketers. Sir John Stirling Maxwell provided an area of land on the Pollok estate, rent-free. The footballers, to show their appreciation, took the name of Pollok Juniors FC, and Sir John became their first Honorary President. This original ground was called Haggs Park and was beside Poloc Cricket Club. In fact, the different spellings of the two names Pollok" and "Poloc" were adopted at this time, deliberately, to avoid confusion.

Sir John Stirling Maxwell went on to hold meetings in Pollok House that eventually led to the founding of the National Trust for Scotland in 1931. He also understood the importance of having green spaces within a city, especially in an industrialised one such as Glasgow, and perhaps this understanding explains his determination to protect the Pollok Estate but also to give the people of Glasgow free access to it, which he undertook in 1911.

POLOC CRICKET CLUB.

GROUND—SHAWHOLM, POLLOK POLICIES.

This club was formed in 1879. The ground, a portion of which is laid out for Lawn Tennis, is beautifully situated within the Pollok Policies, and is close to Pollokshaws Station. The present membership is 109. Annual subscription £1 1s.; lady members 5s.

Office-bearers for 1887:—

Hon. President, A. Crum, Esq., of Thornliebank; president, John Anderson, Pollokshields; hon. secretary, Mr. William Frazer, 5 Renton terrace, Crosshill; hon. treasurer, Mr. Ord A. Anderson, 51 Miller street, Glasgow; hon. match secretary, 1st eleven, Mr. George W. Gillies, 18 Regent Park square, Strathbungo; hon. match secretary, 2nd eleven, Mr. William E. Fulton, 17 Minerva street, Glasgow; hon. match secretary, Tennis, Mr. John Anderson, 3 Dalmeny terrace, Pollokshields.

I never played cricket for Poloc, unlike my father and siblings who had, but unlike them, I have had different experiences of the Pollok Estate. On leaving school, my first employment was as a greenkeeper at Pollok Golf Course and from there went on to work for the National Trust for Scotland as a trainee groundsman. A few years later, I even spent a number of summers as the groundsman for Poloc Cricket Club.

The intertwining of random strands of coincidence slowly join together to form a tapestry that depicts a never previously interpreted story.

My father never really spoke of his war experiences and seemed reluctant to do so. All we ever heard was that he had been in France in 1940 and 1944, he had met my mother in the Faroes in 1942 and that he had seen unspeakable sights in concentration camps in 1945.

The only story he really told was of his good fortune at how he had received his officer's commission at the selection board. I had always thought the tale to be anecdotal, but I now realise that the tale is indeed true and probably representative of the "Big House" cricket equation.

On interview at the Selection Board, my father was asked a number of questions by very senior officers:

Q: "So Young, do you play any sports?"
A: "Yes Sir. Football and cricket, Sir."
Q: "Football? Would that be rugby football or association soccer Young?"
A: "Soccer Sir."
Q: "Who do you play soccer for Young?"
A: "I do not play for anyone now Sir but I used to play for Queen's Park as a youth Sir."
Q: "Queen's Park? The Corinthian side?"
A: "Yes Sir."
Q: "Who do you play cricket for Young?"
A: "I play for Poloc Cricket Club Sir."
Q: "Would that be the Poloc Cricket Club in the grounds of my good friend Sir John Stirling Maxwell's estate?"
A: "Yes Sir."
"Thank you Young. That will be all."
"Yes Sir. Thank you Sir."

When the results of the selection board were announced a few days later, he was the only candidate that had passed.

Poloc's Remarkable Juniors

I was rummaging in my attic, looking for a particular photograph that I knew I had but couldn't locate, when I happened to stumble across a treasure. In a box containing some of my late father's effects, I found a plain brown envelope with the legend "Young 1931" written on the front. I opened the envelope and there were two differently sized photographs inside. As I attempted to extract the larger of the two photographs from the envelope, a folded slip of paper, almost tissue-like, fell out and landed at my feet. I picked up the paper and carefully opened it. I was not expecting to find what I was eventually going to read. The folded piece of paper turned out to be a carbon copy of a letter that had been written concerning the publication of the Shawlands Academy magazine in 1966. It was four pages long, and was in fact, a brief resume of the cricket team that featured in the attached photographs.

The photographs were of the Shawlands Academy Cricket First Eleven taken in May 1931. The contents of the attached letter provided succinct typed portraits of the players and a brief analysis of the lives that each of them went on to have from the taking of this photograph. It explained what happened to them after they had left school, the impact that the Second World War would have on most of them and what each member of the team had achieved after their military service was complete. For most, it was their life stories of their next thirty-five years compressed into a handful of lines.

But there are two stark facts to appreciate when studying this picture along with the information provided. The first of which is that all these young cricketers resided, were schooled and played sport on land originally owned by the Pollok Estate which had been given up and then built upon to accommodate the progress generated by Glasgow's rise as an industrial powerhouse. The second fact is that every single one of these young cricketers would have had to have been a member of Poloc Cricket Club within the Pollok Estate to be able to have the honour to represent their school and to be in this picture, and it was a choice they had all willingly made.

It does make you appreciate that while in your youth, your whole life lies before you and your destiny is determined by the choices that you make along the way. But in the case of most of this team, although having originally chosen their respective paths, an unforeseen interruption ultimately controlled and decided their remaining futures as a global conflict affected them all accordingly and their destinies.

Back Row Standing:
Ewan Matthews, Harold Cuthbert

Mid Row Standing:
John Fraser, R. Simpson, Keir Hardie, W.T. Warnock, Andrew Gibb

Front Row Sitting:
Donald Cameron, George Heavenor (Captain), W. Brown (Science Master), William Young (Vice Captain), T. Davidson

Ewan Matthews:
On leaving school, attended Glasgow University where he achieved an Honours Degree in Arts. He was killed in a motor accident in 1936.

Harold Cuthbert:
Rose to the rank of Lieut. Colonel in the regular army and retired in 1964. Continued to play adult cricket for Poloc and for the Army Corp and had the distinction of twice playing at Lords.

John Fraser:
Attended Glasgow University and became a Minister in the Church of Scotland.

R.Simpson:
No details known. He attended the school for only a short period having moved up from England.

Keir Hardie:
Is the nephew of the founder of the Labour Party and his father David, was the Labour Party M.P. for the Glasgow Rutherglen constituency. He joined the Royal Air Force and rose to the rank of Squadron Leader. He is now in charge of physical education at Marr College in Troon and is also a Justice of the Peace.

WT Warnock:
Joined the Post Office from school and during the war years took up lecture duties at the Post Office Engineering School in Birmingham and is now Telephone Manager for the west of Scotland.

Andrew Gibb:
During the war, he served in the Royal Air Force in the Middle East operating in 'hush hush' Mobile Desert Task Force activities. Currently the Depute Town Chamberlain for Hamilton.

Donald Cameron:
At the beginning of the War he joined the Submarine Services of the Royal Nay serving on H.M.S. Sturgeon. In 1942, along with two other officers, he formed the spearhead of the Midget Submarine Service and took over command as 1st Lieut. He was in charge of the attack on the German battleship Tirpitz in September 1943 in the Alden Fjord in Norway. His craft was spotted but he pressed home his attack knowing that when he was alongside the Tirpitz, there would be no chance of escape. He affixed his charges underneath the battleship, sank his own craft and was captured. The charges exploded and the battleship was extensively damaged. He was a prisoner of war in Germany until the end of the conflict.
Donald Cameron was awarded the Victoria Cross for his courage and remained in the Royal Navy after the war.
He died suddenly in Portsmouth in 1964 from a heart attack.

George Heavenor:
On leaving school, he trained to be a dental surgeon. Served with the Royal Air Force and did important research on the effects of high altitudes on gums, teeth and dentures.

William Young:

On leaving school entered insurance and joined the Territorial Army in 1938 rising to the rank of Lt. Colonel in command of the 6/7th Bn. of The Cameronians (Scottish Rifles). He is a member of Lloyds, Fellow of the Corporation of Insurance Brokers and serves on the Board of Management of the Glasgow Royal Infirmary and the Princess Louise Scottish Hospital for Limbless Sailors and Soldiers.

T. Davidson:

On leaving school he joined the firm of Glen & Davidson Ltd and is now Director and Secretary of the firm. During the war he served as a Company Sergeant Major in Field Marshall Montgomery's H.Q. in the 21st Army Group.

Creation, Contact and Connection

All through human history, there are myths and fables relating to spiders that are used as analogies in a great many tales to represent acts of patience or persistence, resilience, or more often than not, the folly of man and his pride.

In ancient Egypt, the spider was revered as a result of association with the deity Neith, who was worshipped as the spinner and weaver of destiny, whereas in Greek mythology, the folly of pride is detailed in the story of Arachne and Athena, where although Arachne's undoubted skill as a weaver was not in dispute, her continued arrogance and conceit angered the goddess Athena who turned her into a spider for all to remember.

In Africa, the spider is considered as the creation deity Anansi and 'spider tales', especially those relating to mischief and the passage of man, made their way into the fables and folklore of the Americas and the West Indies, as allegorical stories that teach the listener a moral lesson.

In Scotland, its most famous spider story features Robert the Bruce, who, in hiding from English oppressors, finds himself lying in a cave at Rachrin, utterly transfixed at the repeated efforts of a spider trying to spin a web. Time after time the spider fails to fasten its thread to create the starting line of its web. The spider eventually prevails in its efforts and Robert the Bruce resolves to try again in his own attempts to free a nation. "If at first you do not succeed, try and try again."

Interestingly, this story only appears in the Scottish mentality with the writings of Sir Walter Scott and a book published in 1827 called *"Tales of A Grandfather being Stories Taken from Scottish History"*.

It is a fabulous story and known all around the world, however, the original analogous story was probably written about Robert the Bruce's close ally, Sir James "The Black" Douglas, by David Hume of Godscroft (1560 – 1630) in his *The History of the House of Douglas,* published in 1643.

"...I spied a spider clymbing by his webb to the height of an trie and at 12 several times I perceived his web broke, and the spider fel to the ground. But the 13 tyme he attempted and clambe up the tree..."

Whatever the origin, the story itself is a metaphor for perseverance, resilience and determination to achieve something of value or principle.

The web spinning of a spider is truly synonymous with stories of creation, contact and connection.

But for there to be the creation, contact and connection achieved by these webs, there have to be spiders present.

The experience of Dunlops, Campbells, Buchanans and Findlays; the industry of Bairds, Houldsworths, Dixons and Higginbothams; the complications of an extended family of Maclaes, Ewings, Crums, Ewing Maclaes, Crum Maclaes and Crum Ewings; the patronage of Maxwells, Douglases, Homes, Colquhouns, Stewarts, Montgomeries and Boyles; the ingenuity of Clarks, Coats, Tennents and Thomsons…

These are the names of some of the "spiders" that created a web that Glasgow flourished in. Their creations, through contact and connection, along with their contributions, not only to a city, but a nation and a United Kingdom, have been overlooked and unappreciated for far too long.

But not anymore.

St. Rollox Cricket Club - Rosebank Park

St. Rollox Cricket Club was a club to be found in the former grounds of Rosebank House. An early owner of Rosebank House was a John Colin Dunlop, Advocate, who was for many years a Sheriff of Renfrewshire, who sold the property to David Dale in 1801.

David Dale had begun life as a weaver and became a very successful trader in French yarns. He diversified his business skills into manufacturing and along with his son-in-law, the great reform-minded industrialist Robert Owen, founded the cotton mills at New Lanark.

After David Dale's death, Rosebank was acquired by the Caledonian Railway Company, who offered two tracts of the estate for sale. One was bought by Thomas Gray Buchanan and the other, including the house, by Messrs. Dunlop of the Clyde Iron Works.

Part of the estate was St. Rollox, which became the location of many foundries, iron works, potteries and glass works. Railway engines were made and transported around the world from here. The Caledonia Railway operated a coal depot for the Thrashbush Colleries at St. Rollox and a Robert Baird, coal master and coke manufacturer ran a successful business nearby.

St. Rollox Cotton-spinning and Power-loom Weaving Works, 21 Garngad road; A. & A. Galbraith, office, 123 Hope street.
St. Rollox Cricket Club; Ground, Rosebank park, Garngad road; John Morrison, 8 Black street, secretary.
St. Rollox Fire Engine Station, 27 Parliamentary rd.
St. Rollox Foundry Co., ironfounders and engineers, 236 Castle street.
St. Rollox Iron Works, Charles street, St. Rollox. (See Glasgow Iron Co).

East-End Cricket Club - Helenvale Park, High Belvidere

East-End Cricket Club enjoyed around 40 years of patronage until the playing fields themselves were consumed by the needs of Glasgow's industrialisation.

Belvidere House was originally the home of Robert McNair, the proprietor of Robert M'Nair & Son of the Gallowgate Sugar Works. The house was sold in 1813 to Mr. Mungo Nutter Campbell who was a partner in the firm of Messrs. John Campbell Senior & Co., West India merchants, Buchanan Street, Glasgow. Mungo Nutter Campbell went on to become the Lord Provost of Glasgow in 1824.

In 1832, David Wardrop bought the estate and wrought the coal to be found there. David Wardrop was a partner in the firm of Wardrop & Harvie, specialist power loom cloth manufacturers in Glasgow.

Belvidere changed hands and became the property of the noted ironmaster, Robert Miller and then onto John S. Miller of the nearby Springfield dye-works.

In 1870, Belvidere House was eventually sold to the Board of Health of Glasgow for the sum of £17,000 and became the site of a hospital specialising in fevers and infectious diseases.

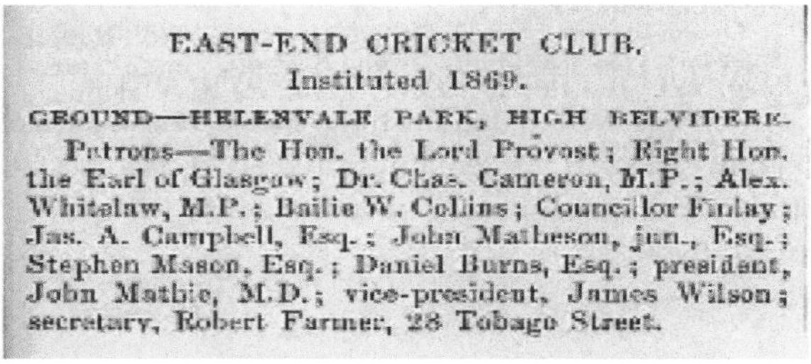

EAST-END CRICKET CLUB.

Institututed 1869.

GROUND—HELENVALE PARK, HIGH BELVIDERE.

Patrons—The Hon. the Lord Provost; Right Hon. the Earl of Glasgow; Dr. Chas. Cameron, M.P.; Alex. Whitelaw, M.P.; Bailie W. Collins; Councillor Finlay; Jas. A. Campbell, Esq.; John Matheson, jun., Esq.; Stephen Mason, Esq.; Daniel Burns, Esq.; president, John Mathie, M.D.; vice-president, James Wilson; secretary, Robert Farmer, 28 Tobago Street.

Possilpark Cricket Club

The Campbells of Possil were a family whose social and commercial standing was derived from successful tobacco and sugar interests in the Americas and the West Indies. The family business was John Campbell Senior & Co., who brought great wealth to the city and as a family, enjoyed spending it, whether on business interests, lifestyles or property.

Possil House was far enough away from the noise and smoke of the city to become a home in the country. It was surrounded by trees and featured beautiful gardens with grassy slopes running towards a central clear water lake.

At its peak, Possil was viewed *"as delightful and retired a residence as any in the country"*, but yet again, the expansionist tentacles of Glasgow's industrialisation reached the estate.

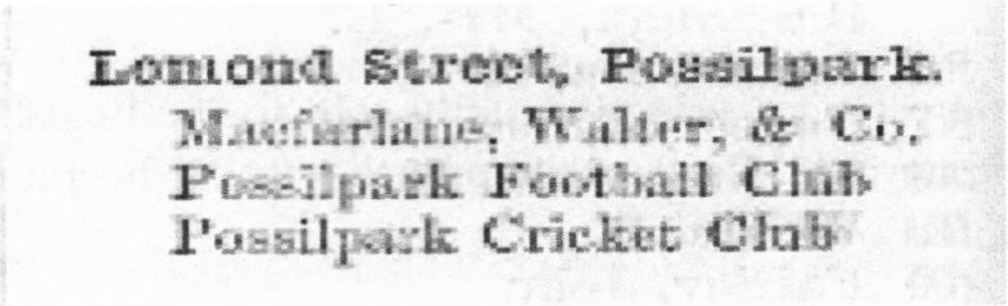

Lomond Street, Possilpark.
Macfarlane, Walter, & Co.
Possilpark Football Club
Possilpark Cricket Club

It was feued to Walter M'Farlane & Co., a company operating iron foundries in Glasgow, who proceeded to demolish the house, remove the trees, build a spacious foundry, and in the remaining 100 acres of the estate, laid out streets, erected dwelling houses and created the new suburb of Possil Park for the city of Glasgow.

Easterhill Cricket Club

Easterhill House belonged to the Findlays whose familial connections, through marriage, were with Campbells, Dunlops and Buchanans, the proprietors of the neighbouring estates to be found in the east of the city.

The Findlays were heavily involved as partners in the Ship Bank of Glasgow who managed the finances of Glasgow's tobacco lords. The six founding partners were William Macdowall of Castle Semple, Andrew Buchanan of Drumpellier, Allan Dreghorn of Ruchill, Colin Dunlop, Robert Dunlop and Alexander Houston.

The Ship Bank merged with the Glasgow Banking Company to become the Glasgow and Ship Bank. In 1843, the Union Bank of Scotland purchased The Glasgow and Ship Bank, and specialised in the administration of finance to industries as diverse as textiles, iron, coal, shipbuilding and railways.

The Union Bank of Scotland eventually became part of the Bank of Scotland.

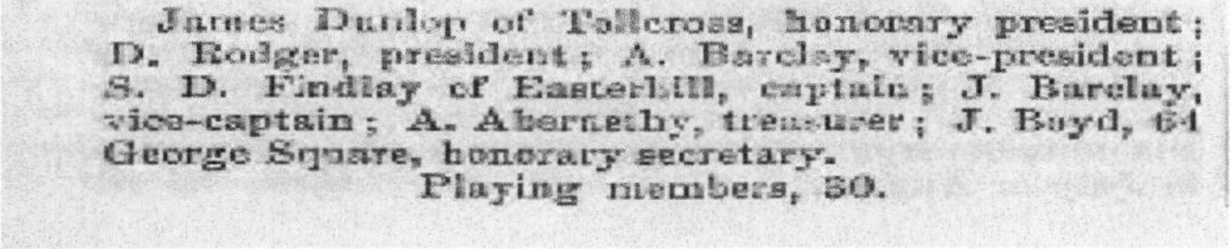

EASTERHILL CRICKET CLUB.

GROUND—EASTERHILL.

James Dunlop of Tollcross, honorary president; D. Rodger, president; A. Barclay, vice-president; S. D. Findlay of Easterhill, captain; J. Barclay, vice-captain; A. Abernethy, treasurer; J. Boyd, 64 George Square, honorary secretary.

Playing members, 30.

Tolcross Cricket Club

In the grounds of Tollcross House, Tolcross Cricket Club operated within its policies. Tollcross House was originally the home of a Colin Dunlop, who after the failure of the family business of tobacco, turned to the profits of industrialisation that would be gained from the mineral rich deposits to be found on his various estates.

Colin Dunlop was the grandson of Marion Buchanan of Drumpellier and was the owner of the Clyde Ironworks that mined the lands of Garnkirk, Carmyle and Rosebank. He was a keen Whig politician, and one of the great leaders of the Reform party in Glasgow. On his death in 1835, his estate was succeeded by his nephew, James Dunlop, who was also the proprietor of the Clyde Ironworks.

When James Dunlop died in 1893, the estate passed to the Bank of Scotland. In 1894, Robert Gourlay, Glasgow manager of the Bank of Scotland, wrote to the Lord Provost of Glasgow: *"Owing to the death of Mr James Dunlop of Tollcross..."* the estate was being laid out for feuing, but it was suggested that the mansion house and policies would be useful as a public park, it being *"beautifully situated, nicely wooded and well laid off with carriage drive and foot walks. It is a made place and seems specially adapted for a Public Park. Indeed it is now the only vacant space left to the east of the city, suitable for such"*. This is an opportunity of *"acquiring another beautiful and most valuable lung to the rapidly extending city"*.

TOLCROSS CRICKET CLUB.

GROUND.—TOLCROSS POLICIES.

Honorary President, James Dunlop, Esq. of Tolcross; president, Hugh Tennent, jun., Esq. of Wellshot; captain, George J. Dunlop, Esq., Fullerton House, Tollcross; vice-captain, James Brown; treasurer, Charles Simpson; committee, Messrs. M. Wilson, W. Primrose, J. H. Brown, G. J. Dunlop, and J. Wilson; secretary, James Wilson, 37 Taylor Street, Glasgow.

There followed four years of wrangling with the Bank of Scotland over the future of the estate, and in 1897, Glasgow Corporation purchased the land, including the "Big House" for £29.000, and turned the estate into what is now the splendid Tollcross Park and it is a credit to the city of Glasgow to have preserved such a place for its population to enjoy.

Eglinton Castle

Eglinton Castle was near to Kilwinning. It was the ancient seat of the Montgomeries, the Earls of Eglinton. It was a vast estate that had huge natural resources to draw upon. A combination of deposits such as coal, ironstone, fireclay, limestone, and sand-stone provided great wealth, and as such, funded lavish construction projects and developments in and around the estate.

By 1853, much land was purchased, drained and then leased to the Bairds o Gartsherrie and the "Eglinton Iron Works" were born. Such was the richness of the land and the scale of the mining operation, miners rows were built at Bartonholm, Corsehill, Snodgrass, Blacklands, Sourlie, Dirrans, Longford, Annick Lodge, Nethermains, Shipmill, Fergushill, Doura and Benslie. The Eglinton Iron Works village itself had a population of over 1000 souls by 1874.

The castle was constantly being added to with extensions and improvements, and elsewhere within the estate, stables, an indoor sports hall, gazebos, cottages, lodges and gate-houses were built. A substantial cricket pavilion was provided complete with a large cricket ground and extensive practice facilities. Two English cricket professionals were employed to provide tuition to the local community.

EGLINTON CLUB.

Patron, The Right Hon. the Earl of Eglinton and Winton
President, James B. Paton
Captain, James Thomson *Vice-Captain*, John Paterson
Secretary, A. B. Young *Treasurer*, William Wilson

The income to the estate derived from just the mineral royalties alone totalled £9,500 per year, the equivalent of around £900,000 in 2012. An even more substantial sum to consider was the further £37,000 per year that was ingathered from the various rents. That sum would be worth around £2,500,000 in 2012.

However, a final construction project undermined a family and its prosperity and standing in the area. With what appeared to be bottomless expenditure on the development of the Ardrossan Harbour and the Glasgow, Paisley and Ardrossan Canal, the combination of death duties and other tax levies took their toll, and by 1926, after nearly 600 years of stewardship, the "big house" was de-roofed and the 1,400 acres of the estate that remained in the family ownership were sold to Robert Howie of Dunlop for the paltry sum of £24,400.

Although most buildings on the estate were in a dilapidated condition, the lands were adaptable to efficient agricultural management.

The transformation of what had been one of the most admired country estates in Scotland began in 1948 when Robert Howie & Sons began to exact timber extraction on a massive scale. There followed the establishment and improvement of the policies by the introduction of a substantial dairy farm.

By the mid 1960s, the town of Irvine was spreading into the farmland that was once the Eglinton Estate.

This "invasion" of building into the estate was further augmented by the designation of Irvine as a New Town, a place full of new opportunity and employment.

A final irony to the story of Eglinton is with the purchase of the estate by Robert Howie of Dunlop. The Howies were passionate cricketers themselves and were great patrons of their own club in Dunlop. Countless generations of west coast cricketers enjoyed playing there on trips made all the more appetising with the sure knowledge of sampling the famous cream teas. The highlight, when batting, would be trying to hit a passing train with the ball, yet, by the mid 1990s, Dunlop was also gone, with the only reminder left of a cricket ground being a forlorn scoreboard in a sea of waist-high grass, waiting for a match that will never be, to commence.

A final reminder of the pomp and splendour associated with the Eglinton Estate and its promotion of "Big House" cricket in the west of Scotland leads to the provenance of the existence of physical evidence to support the theory.

It is perhaps the oldest club cricket trophy in the world, and the story of the Eglinton Jug is one that has been hidden from the greater cricket community for far too long.

The Eglinton Jug is in the possession of Ayr Cricket Club and its importance in the concept of "Big House" cricket has been lost for generations to consider.

In 1866, the Earl of Eglinton and Winton commissioned a trophy to be made for an inter-club cup competition involving the cricket clubs in Ayrshire. The final would be played on the magnificent cricket ground to be found within the Eglinton Castle estate. The trophy would be retained in perpetuity by any club that won the trophy in three successive years.

The trophy cost £40.00 and it is a gold leaf wine jug partnered with two goblets.

The competition began in 1867 and the county of Ayrshire was split into two regional groups. In the north, clubs such as Ardeer, Auchenharvie, Dalry, Fergusson Hurlford, Glengarnock, Kilbirnie Thistle, Kilmarnock Junior, Perecton, Portland, Parkend and Shaws Kilmarnock took part.

In the south, clubs such as Ayr Thistle, Ayr, Ayr Eglinton, Lugar, Mauchline, Girvan Ailsa, Maybole and Cumnock participated.

The winners were:

1867 Irvine Eglinton

1868 Ayr

1869 Ayr Eglinton

1870 Ayr

1871 Ayr

1872 Ayr Eglinton

1873 Ayr

1874 Ayr

1875 Ayr

Ayr won the trophy outright in 1875 when they beat Cumnock in the final.

The competition sadly lapsed thereafter, and the fortunes of the game itself were in serious trouble until a revival began in the early 1880s.

The Eglinton Jug – perhaps the oldest inter-club trophy in the world?

Uddingston

A cricket club was provided for the village of Uddingston by the major landowner of the district, the Earl of Home, in 1883. There had previously been a short-lived cricket club called Bothwell that had been created in 1869.

The Earl lived at Bothwell House and provided land in the neighbouring village of Uddingston on the proviso that the club *"was a place where artisans and professional men could meet and participate in a common interest that bound them, namely cricket,"* and that this was to be the major core aspect of the club and that it should be open to all with priority given to the local community and those that lived within it.

The mansion itself suffered from mining subsidence, and after a fire in 1919, deteriorated badly. It was eventually demolished in 1926. In 1930, The Earl of Home gifted nearby Bothwell Castle to the state and is now maintained by Historic Scotland. The surrounding lands were sold off for building development that would go on to become part of the greater communities of Uddingston and Bothwell.

Unlike in adulthood, Uddingston was a favourite ground to visit in childhood. I would meet and play with various children with surnames like Smith and McGurk and we would explore and rampage around the policies at Bothwell, get up to all sorts of mischief and also play bounce games of cricket.

I knew that if I was being taken by my father to Uddingston, that we would end up in the Tunnocks Tea Room where I would be treated to a fizzy drink and a jam and cream crumpet and placed near the shop's resident mynah bird, Jake, and I would be enthralled listening to him chirping away with his "patter", full of rude words and lurid phrases. I remember it all so well.

A fact that many at Bothwell Castle Policies do not actually know is that on Monday 30th May 1983, at the age of 17, I played in the Uddingston Cricket Club's Centenary Celebration cricket match.

I have cleared my diary for Monday 30th May 2033 and I am available!

Ferguslie

Ferguslie House was best known as the home of Mr Thomas Coats of the well-known firm of J and P Coats, thread manufacturers in Paisley. It was built in 1828 and was situated across the main road from the giant Ferguslie Mills complex. Thomas, and his brother Peter, took over the running of their father's Ferguslie threadworks, J and P Coats, in the 1830s. Under their combined leadership, they were responsible for the rapid expansion of J and P Coats during the 19th Century company as it became one of the world's leading thread manufacturers.

Thomas's son, who would become Sir Thomas Glen-Coats, was born in Ferguslie House. He assumed the additional surname of Glen in 1894, and received the honour of a baronetcy in the same year. He was elected as the Liberal Member of Parliament for West Renfrewshire in 1906, and became the Lord Lieutenant of Renfrewshire in 1908.

Of Sir Thomas Glen-Coats three children, Lady Glen Coats was a respected political campaigner and Thomas Glen-Coats was a naval architect who designed and produced race-winning yachts, the most famous of which was winning Gold for Great Britain with the "Hera" in the 1908 Olympics.

The Scottish National Antarctic Expedition of 1902-1904, named a one-hundred-and-fifty mile stretch of the coast of the Antarctic continent as "Coats Land" after the family who were the main financiers of the trip.

The Ferguslie Threadworks Cricket Club was founded in 1887 as a cricket club for the workers in the nearby threadworks.

Ferguslie Thread Works Cricket Club.

Instituted 1887.—Grounds, Meikleriggs.

Patrons—J. & P. Coats, Limited.

Hon. President—P. H. Coats. *Hon. Vice-Presidents*—P. M. Coats, J. Reid, W. Ross, and N. Buchanan.

President—D. M. Feddie. *Vice-President*—J. Wylie.

Captain—Geo. Jaap. *Vice-Captain*—Jas. Boyd.

Secretary and Treasurer—Allan Scott, 17 Maxwellton street.

Ferguslie's initial fixtures would be against sides such as St Mirren, Carnbrae, Johnstone, Bridge of Weir, Lenzie, RVB Greenock, Coatbridge Thistle, Cessnock, Dalry, Houston and Poloc.

The strength and quality of Ferguslie's opposition increased over the following seasons, as did crowds of over 3,000 to watch their local heroes as per the opening match of the 1895 season when Sir Thomas Glen-Coats welcomed his good friend Sir David Carrick Robert Carrick Buchanan and his Drumpellier Cricket Club, to Meikleriggs.

James Welford joined the club as the professional having played First Class cricket for Warwickshire. But cricket was not Welford's only sport. He was also a professional footballer who had played for Aston Villa and other clubs. He also played for Celtic and was the first Englishman to have won both an English Football Association Cup Final medal and a Scottish Football Association Cup Final medal.

James Welford

Aston Villa

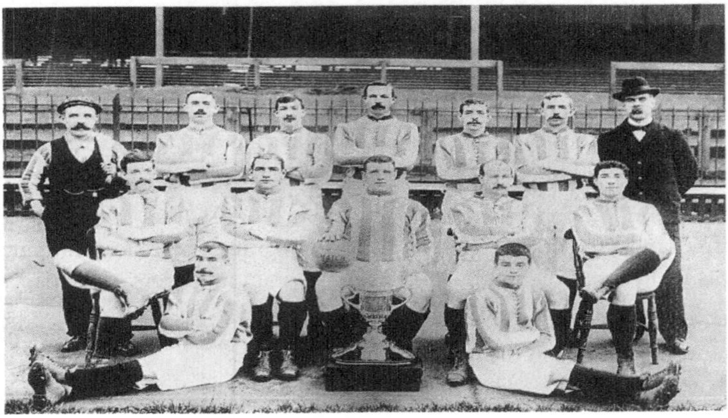

Celtic 1899

It Was More Than Just Being a Renfrewshire Troika

The big three Renfrewshire clubs are Greenock, Kelburne and Ferguslie with links to each other that are not immediately obvious. The playing of cricket in the Greenock and Paisley area is older than people actually appreciate. In Greenock, for example, there were fledgling clubs operating out of the Wellington Park in 1852.

The Victoria Cricket Club—Cricket Ground, Wellington Park—Henry Dickie, Chairman; James Dumbreck, Secretary; Donald M'Dougall, Treasurer; Robert Walker, Captain.

The Grosvenor Cricket Club—Meets once a month—Chairman, Matthew Campbell; Secretary, John C. Smith; Treasurer, John Smith; Captain, Thomas Connacher. Cricket Ground, Wellington Park.

By 1858, a Greenock Cricket Club was in existence and playing out of Wellington Park.

The Greenock Cricket Club—Meets once a month—George MacIldowie, President; John F. Lawrie, Vice-President and Secretary; Thomas G. Lamont, Treasurer; Robert Walker, Captain; with six of a Committee.

And by 1862, a further cricket club, namely Octavia, was in existence at Wellington Park.

The Greenock Cricket Club.—Cricket Ground, Wellington Park.—President, James Paterson; Treasurer, William M'Ildowie; Secretary, Donald M'Dougall; Captain, Peter Blair.

The Octavia Cricket Club.—Cricket Ground, Wellington Park.—William Tierney, President: Hugh Stewart, Treasurer; C. M'Culloch, Secretary; with six of Committee of Management.

The Greenock Cricket Club, that celebrated its 150th anniversary in 2012, appears as an instituted body in 1862 at Glen Park in the grounds of the Glen House.

Greenock Cricket Club—Instituted 1862.—Patron, Sir Michael R. Shaw Stewart, Bart. The office-bearers for the year are as follows:—President, William O. Leitch; vice-president, Robert S. Scott; treasurer, H. B. Dickie; secretary, John Steven; assistant-secretary, John Hinmers; captain, John Steven; committee, Wm. Keay, John Lang, junr., D. B. M'Kelvie, T. Wallace, R. Murray, D. Jenkins, D. Ferguson, J. Agnew. Ground, Glen Park. Annual subscription, one guinea. Honorary members, 10s 6d.

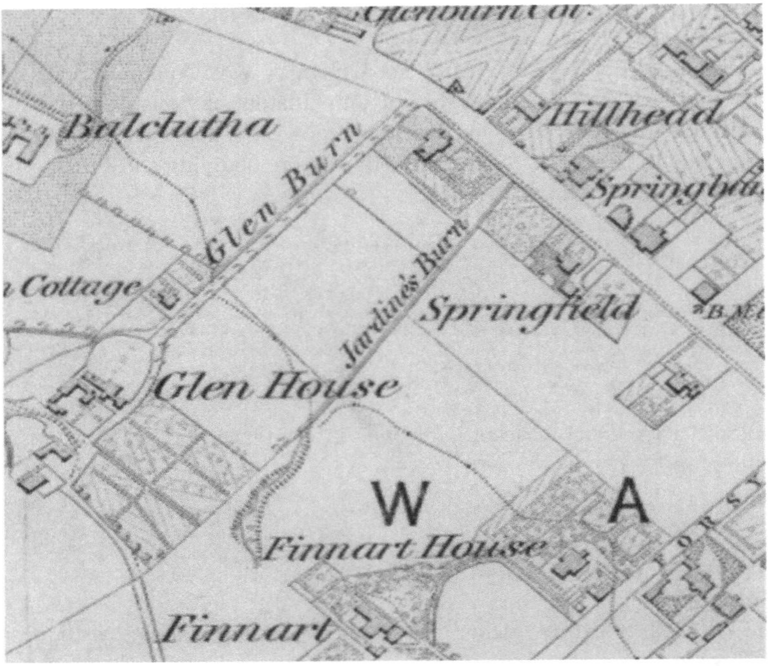

By 1872, Greenock Cricket Club was an established part of the fabric of the town.

Greenock Cricket Club—Instituted 1862.—Patron, Sir Michael R. Shaw Stewart, Bart. The office-bearers for the year are as follows:—President, James Stewart, of Garvocks; vice-president, M. J. Martin; secretary, 8 John C. Black; treasurer, W. R. Fraser; captain, John Steven; committee, J. Lang, junr., John Somerville, Thomas A. Aitken, James Ferguson, Archibald Lumsdane, James Grieve, J. H. Gardiner, James Newton junr., and D. L. MacAdam. Ground, Glen Park. Annual subscription, one guinea. Honorary members, one guinea.

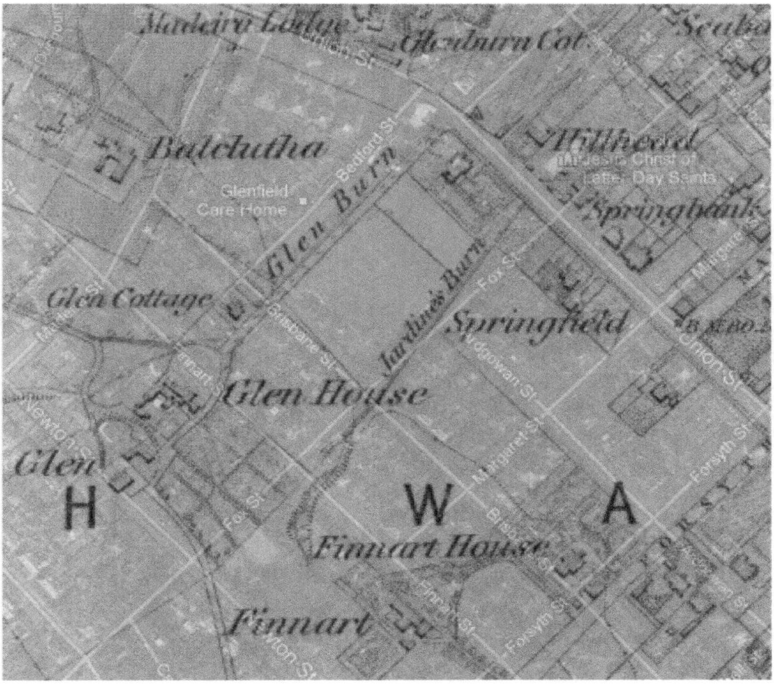

Greenock Cricket Club enjoyed the patronage of Colonel Sir Michael Robert Shaw-Stewart of Ardgowan and Blackhall, who had married in 1852, Lady Octavia Grosvenor, daughter of the 2nd Marquess of Westminster

He was the Member of Parliament for Renfrewshire from 1855 to 1865, Lord Lieutenant of Renfrewshire from 1869 to 1903 and Grand Master of the Grand Lodge of Scotland from 1873 to 1882.

This family of Shaw Stewart of Blackhall and Greenock, was directly descended from Sir John Stewart, one of the natural sons of Robert III, who had received three charters of lands in Ardgowan, Blackhall, and Auchingoun, all to found in the County of Renfrewshire. The territorial title of Blackhall referred to the house that had been the principal seat of the family in Paisley.

Blackhall was inhabited until around 1840 and thereafter it became a cattle shed. The Shaw Stewart family donated the building to the Burgh of Paisley in 1940, but deterioration as a result of the elements, vandalism and neglect resulted in it being scheduled for demolition in 1978. The good people of Paisley were outraged at the plans for demolition which delayed matters and the house was eventually saved in 1982 when it passed into private ownership.

The new owners renovated the house and created a home comprising a great hall, dining room, four bedrooms and a stone spiral staircase. The entrance is now guarded by stone lions salvaged from the demolished Ferguslie House and the dormer windows are surmounted by a stone thistle, also from Ferguslie House, and a stone rose from the Ferguslie Mill buildings.

A link between the big three Renfrewshire clubs centres on Blackhall Manor. Greenock's patron was Colonel Sir Michael Robert Shaw-Stewart of Ardgowan and Blackhall, parts of the Ferguslie House and the Ferguslie Mill were used in its reconstruction in the 1980s and Blackhall was the original home of Kelburne Cricket Club, a cricket club that been founded in 1860.

Kelburne remained at Blackhall until 1898. Kelburne had been informed in 1897 by the local council that the ground at Blackhall was required for building development. The committee at Kelburne actively sought a new home for their club which they secured and moved to a bespoke facility at Whitehaugh for the 1899 season.

But Kelburne had the good fortune in being able to deal with an unexpected announcement that possibly affected their continuance as a club. They could draw upon the experiences of what had previously happened to another Paisley cricket club, and implement a working strategy plan that secured a new ground. The answers to their future had been by gained by looking at the past.

Paisley Thistle Cricket Club was instituted in 1851 and their ground was to found at Greenhill. By the 1870s, Paisley Thistle was not only the cricket club of note in Renfrewshire, it was one of the cricketing super-powers of the west of Scotland.

It enjoyed the serious patronage of gentlemen whose experience and involvement with a number of other clubs were evident and there were associations with peers of the realm, Members of Parliament, the military, local politicians, magistrates and respected members of the business community. This club appeared to be on a par, if not a greater standing, with established clubs such as the West of Scotland and Drumpellier.

Paisley Thistle Cricket Club was disbanded in 1878 as their Greenhill ground was required for building projects. The local community had been extremely vocal expressing their outrage at this forced closure and the local newspapers, such as the Paisley Daily Express, were vehement in their condemnation of Paisley Thistle's demise and what the impact would be on the playing and enjoyment of cricket in the local community. The newspapers went as far as to even allude that the rise of the new sport, association football, was driving people away from cricket and effectively killing the *"ancient and national game"*.

The death of a club, irrespective of the sport it played, is never a pleasant experience. To those involved with the club and its members, it is comparable to having to cope with, and fill, the void created by the loss of a loved one.

Something that has always been there, in the good times and the bad, is gone forever and all that is left are the memories and reminiscences to hold dear and comfort you at a time of anguish.

In a modern context, the death of a cricket club has been a fairly common event in the west of Scotland. Since the mid 1980s there have been around fifty such demises but the reasons for their passing have been varied.

The teachers' strikes in the 1970s, compounded with the Munn & Dunning

Report of the 1980s, led to many sports in Scotland suffering with their promotion in local schools. The input of teachers and game-masters were somewhat curtailed by the changes to their employment conditions and was instrumental in removing extra-curricular sport in the schools - cricket was the major casualty.

A succession of changes to the country's licensing laws has also had a huge impact on the income of many different types of sports and social club. Many cricket clubs, for example, traditionally had large non-playing memberships who availed themselves of the facilities and access to refreshment that they became entitled to when joining. The extending of opening hours in public houses, especially on a Sunday, have had a negative effect on bar turnovers in clubs and has also led to a fall in memberships of these same clubs.

Sometimes the pressure to sell off a piece of land to opportunist developers became a temptation too far for many clubs, where the club in question would hope to cancel its financial deficit or emburdenment with an instant cash injection via a quick sale. It has worked for some, but in the main, this course of action has been a type of secondary prophylaxis where clubs attempt to protect themselves against their worsening situation instead of seeking a cure and recover properly over time. It has very rarely worked and cricket, tennis and bowling clubs are perfect examples. When you look around Glasgow, or any other city for that matter, what were once sports facilities are now, sadly, shops or residential properties.

Capital building projects and ground developments have also been contributory factors to the demise of a sports club. Once the project has been delivered, the priorities that led to its initial planning and implementation have changed. The demands or the perceived benefits have decreased and the subsequent implemented change has been a futile exercise in attempting to increase membership, revenue and participation. You can remove, repair and replace the stucco on the carapace of the club all you want, but it is what is inside the club and what it offers that are the really important aspects to consider, and if you lose sight of these basic concepts, you become half-roads to Hell, and turning back from eternal damnation is a difficult path to follow.

Society has also changed and many sports are simply instant amusements where participants mainly turn up at a set time, play for a while and then leave. It is probably indicative of people having far greater choice than has ever been available previously. You can choose to do whatever you want, whenever and with whom you want. Unfortunately, the ideals of being a member and what it entails and also contributing to a club are becoming lost to the sport-playing generation of today.

The worst offenders for the demise of a club are the members themselves. Indifference, apathy, disinterest and complacency skip merrily hand in hand, laughing mockingly, as they head towards oblivion, at the desperate efforts of the few committed volunteers who work tirelessly, and often without reward or gratitude, to run each and every single club. It is far too easy to criticise and condemn these stalwarts for their labours, but without them, and indeed their dedication and loyalty to their club, there would be nothing for the members to enjoy.

It is a pity that many people today would not consider joining and contributing to a club and enjoying everything that a club has to offer and provide.

However, although Paisley Thistle Cricket Club's existence had ceased to be, there would be valuable lessons to be learned from its unfortunate passing. More importantly, the people of Renfrewshire, and especially the good citizens of Paisley, continued to flock to the game of cricket as evidenced by the number of clubs that were in existence 140 years ago.

KELBURNE CRICKET CLUB.

Instituted 1860.

Grounds—Blackhall.
Patron, The Earl of Glasgow.
President, James Millar, jun., Adelphi House.
Treasurer, T. Shanks, jun., Johnstone.
Secretary, Jas. A. D. MacKean.

BELLGROVE CRICKET CLUB.

Instituted 1865.

Grounds—Mossvale.
President, Matthew Rowand. Vice-President, Joseph Bryce.
Treasurer, James Clark.
Secretary, John F. M'Leod, 54 High street.
General Committee:

Matthew Rowand,	Joseph Bryce,
James Clark,	William Pyatt,

John F. M'Leod.
Match Committee:
Matthew Rowand, Joseph Bryce, John F. M'Leod.

PAISLEY THISTLE CRICKET CLUB.

Instituted 1851.

Grounds—Greenhill.

PATRONS.

Earl of Glasgow.	Peter Coats, Esq.
Right Hon. H. A. Bruce, M.P.	Wm. Wotherspoon, Esq.
H. E. Crum-Ewing, Esq., M.P.	P. Comyn Macgregor, Esq.
General D. Hort Macdowall of Garthland.	Wm. Abercrombie, Esq.,
Provost & Magistrates of Paisley.	Wm. Craw, Esq.

Honorary President, Col. Campbell.
Honorary Vice-Presidents, Major Holms, and Thomas Coats, Esq.
President, A. Tagg. Vice-President, William Foulds.
Treasurer, William Colquhoun.
Secretary, James Lang, 1 Espedair Street.
General Committee.

Messrs R. Rowand	Messrs Wm. Robertson,
W. Weir,	A. M'Lachlan,
J. Andrews,	William Young.
John M'Kenzie,	

Match Committee, M'Lachlan, Colquhoun, and Tagg.
Captain, Alexander Tagg.
Lieutenant, William Colquhoun. Ensign, A. M'Lachlan.
Subscription for Ordinary Members, 12s 6d; Honorary Members 5s.

GLENIFFER CRICKET CLUB.

Instituted 1868.

Grounds—Falside.

Patron, John Polson, Esq., West Mount.

Captain and President, Wm. Glen.

Secretary, Robt. M. Paterson. Treasurer, James Barr.

Committee of Management.

William Glen.	James Barr.
Robert M. Paterson.	David Lang.

James S. Robertson.

GREENWOOD CRICKET CLUB.

Instituted 1860.

Grounds—Blackland Park.

President, M. S. Matheson. Vice-President, Wm. M. Earl.

Treasurer, Wm. S. Lyle. Secretary, James Christie.

Capt., J. B. Morrison. Lieut., Jas. Aitken.

General Committee.

M. S. Matheson,	J. B. Morrison.
Wm. M. Earl,	Jas. Aitken,
Wm. S. Lyle,	Jas. E. Whiriskey.
Jas. Christie,	

Match Committee.

M. S. Matheson, J. B. Morrison, James Christie.

LINSIDE CRICKET CLUB—Grounds, Westmarch.

Instituted 1867.

Patrons.

The Right Hon. the Earl of Glasgow, Col. Campbell, of Blythswood, Col. Holms, M.P., James Dickie, Esq., of Ralston.

President, George Semple. Vice-President, John H. Glover.

Treasurer, Charles Jeffrey. Hon. Secretary, John Parker.

Match Secretary, Allan Young, 44 George Street.

Captain, George Semple. Vice-Captain, Robert Pinkerton.

Second Eleven Captain, James Drennan.

Committee.

Messrs W. S. M'Gee, J. Wilson, and James Walker.

MOSSVALE CRICKET CLUB—Grounds, Nethercommon.

President, John Baird.

Captain, William Monaghan. Vice-Captain, Martin Buchanan.

Treasurer, William M'Houl. Secretary, D. Wilson.

Match Secretary, Wm. A. Stevenson.

Committee—M. Buchanan, P. M'Lachlan, W. A. Stevenson.

St. Mirren Cricket Club.

Grounds—Westmarch.

Patrons—William Dunn, M.P.; Sir Archd. Campbell, Bart., M.P.; T. G. Coats; C. B. Renshaw; J. Stewart Clark; Dr. A. H. Richmond; Geo. M. Young.

Hon. President—James K. Horsburgh. *President*—A. Berry. *Vice-President*—W. Shedden, jun.

Captain 1st Eleven—M. Buchanan. *Captain 2nd Eleven*—James Reid.

Hon. Secretary—Wm. Shedden, 10 Whitehaugh terrace. *Hon. Treasurer*—William Hamilton.

Ferguslie Thread Works Cricket Club.

Instituted 1887.—Grounds, Meikleriggs.

Patrons—J. & P. Coats, Limited.

Hon. President—P. H. Coats. *Hon. Vice-Presidents*—P. M. Coats, J. Reid, W. Ross, and N. Buchanan.

President—D. M. Peddie. *Vice-President*—J. Wylie.

Captain—Geo. Jaap. *Vice-Captain*—Jas. Boyd.

Secretary and Treasurer—Allan Scott, 17 Maxwellton street.

JOHNSTONE CRICKET CLUB.

Patrons—Sir A. C. Campbell, Bart., M.P.; Sir Michael Shaw-Stewart, Bart.; James Finlayson. Colonel T. Glen Coats, Major W. Shanks, A. Coats, G. W. Richardson, William Dunn, M.P., and Rev. William M'Dermott.

Honorary Presidents—G. L. Houstoun and C. Bine Renshaw.

Hon. Vice-Presidents—A. A. Speirs and Provost Armour.

President—Councillor Coates. *Vice-President*—David Burnett.

Captain—D. C. Carmichael. *Vice-Captain*—George Harvey.

Treasurer—Jas. W. Cassells. *Secretary*—George Harvey, 26 Laigh Cartside st.

Committee—John Allison, A. C. Macphail, R. Anderson, R. Campbell, J. Reid, jun., Thomas Jaffrey, and R. Blackburn.

Glasgow – The Importance of a Cricket Playing City.

As the Nineteenth Century unfolded, Glasgow became a city of renown. It was a city that was exporting to the world, and in return, attracted trade and industry, academics, learning and knowledge, expertise, manufacturing ideas and people from every corner of the globe.

While London was the figurehead of an empire and the centre of the known universe, Glasgow became the engine-room that kept it working, relentlessly and unyieldingly. It's appellation as the "Second City of the Empire" was richly deserved and its products bore the legends "Made in Glasgow" or "Clyde Built" and became synonymous as a mark of excellence.

The land-owners and industrialists who profited from Glasgow's expansion were acutely aware of keeping the work-force occupied and healthy. Parks and recreational areas were made available to the citizens and they, in return, took full use of them.

Green fields of Glasgow, such as Flesher's Haugh on Glasgow Green, became the focus points of emerging sports such as rowing and cricket. The first recorded game of cricket to be played in the west of Scotland was between Glasgow University Cricket Club, who originally operated out of Flesher's Haugh, and Perth Cricket Club at Stirling in 1829.

In 1832, Thistle Cricket Club played Albion Cricket Club in one of the first recorded cricket matches in Glasgow, on Flesher's Haugh in Glasgow Green. The match, which started at 5.30am, was broken up by a riot involving the players themselves and then amongst the many spectators that had come along to watch. 180 years on and cricket matches are still played on Glasgow Green and there are also the occasional riots as well, but obviously not as fractious as the original game.

The oldest surviving cricket club in the west of Scotland is Glasgow University Cricket Club, formed in 1829. They also hold the distinction of having constructed, in 1870, the first bespoke purpose-built cricket facility in the world. The pitch was cricket during the summer and football during the winter. The Glasgow University Cricket Club template was used as an example around the globe.

There were many clubs participating by the 1870s, some were just groups of friends, others were work teams and the rest were established clubs. Friendly matches were the norm, and All England and United England touring sides were regular visitors to the Glasgow area. Large crowds would flock to these exhibition games and the popularity of cricket grew.

With the rising popularity of rugby and football, the cricket clubs now found themselves increasingly busier. These "new" sports were attractive to cricketers to play during the winter months, but also increased the memberships of the clubs as well with those either wishing to watch or play.

Clubs like Clydesdale, Vale of Leven and Kilmarnock embraced football and others like Glasgow Academicals embraced rugby. In ten short years, football and rugby had exploded as popular sports and the demand for participation was huge.

As Glasgow grew as a city, the transport infrastructure improved with roads and railways. The rail network was crucial for transportation of goods and materials, and with increasing passengers as a result of the rising population, understandably, the city's demand for adequate housing increased. But when you begin analysis of who owned what and where, too many coincidences occur making "Big House" cricket something more than just a handful of individuals enjoying the promulgation of a sport and its associations. There was a distinct correlation between the growth of the city and ties to the various cricket clubs.

The success of the Industrial Revolution in the Glasgow area created huge changes to the landscape as the demands of innovation, wealth and trade increased the population, the city, its infrastructure and its recreational needs. The businessmen, industrialists and landowners were fully aware of the situation and seemed collectively to embark on a joint venture where through the creation and provision of sport they could maintain their status, continue to accumulate wealth, provide unprecedented employment to an increasing workforce and at the same time extend the pursuit of sport and entertainment and involve the majority of the same workforce by "providing" recreational outlets for them to enjoy.

The creation of the cricket clubs just seems to be coincidental with Glasgow's expansion, but at the same time, these creations are also by the hands of the people who are turning Glasgow into the "Second City of the Empire". The same names keep appearing in the development of Glasgow whether by deeds, business, politics, heavy industry and manufacturing, urbanisation, transport and recreational provision. Some are instantly obvious but most are by subtle involvements, almost anonymously, but collectively, their contributions are the corner-stones of what was eventually created and attributable to Glasgow. It is, in a perverse way, a perfect example of what we could call Scottish capitalism merged with aspects of celtic socialism and all conducted with very altruistic overtones. The wealth and fortune generated by the endeavours of a minority is shared, indirectly, with their fellow man in far more reaching ways than one would appreciate or even anticipate.

This is the "new rich", mainly from humble backgrounds but who have directly benefitted from the industrialisation of their local geography, financing the trappings of a city and providing for the populace. Their contributions, ironically, led to their own social and financial downfalls in many respects, but had they been given the benefit of either foresight or hindsight, I firmly believe that these major protagonists would not have changed a single thing that they did. It was all for the betterment of the people they lived among.

Their choices, their actions, their end results. And we have forgotten that and we should be ashamed.

Everything we experience in life can always be traced back to a point of origin. How something transpires is a direct result of a previous action. The end result is always determined by how we conduct ourselves and by our own hand, but this same end result is also a consequence of choice, and the choices we make along the way do determine the actions that we eventually make and lead to an end result, whether we like it or not.

The continuous development of the city always seemed to involve a number of cricket clubs in some way, along with the patrons and the members.

This looked to be a confirmation of my "Big House" cricket equation - **venue + resources + players = game + networks + opportunity** - and by association, Glasgow's success as a city was in some way connected to this equation, but there needs to be proof that the theory is a valid assumption to make, irrespective of how tenuous the links. Proof of association can be determined via a simplistic identifier: the appearance of a name or a club once is purely down to chance, twice is just merely coincidence, but three or more times is definitive confirmation of an emerging pattern leading to all sorts of further questions and answers.

The important aspect to consider is that I am not claiming that Glasgow was built on the back of the cricket clubs, but suggesting that Glasgow's expansion and development seemed to involve those associated with the cricket clubs and the clubs themselves. The numerous cricket clubs of the time were technically market places where the patrons and the members had become the currency that was being used to buy various commodities, whether it was access to resources, networks and opportunity or in many cases, the ground that the cricket clubs occupied.

The conversations, meetings, inter-actions, associations and accrued contacts that are borne from what happens in and around a cricket match are uniquely specific to the game. It isn't the match itself, it is everything else around it that makes this team game so different to all other sports. Win, lose or draw, as youngsters, you are made to socialise with your opposition and get to know them for the rest of your life. Getting to know them creates networks for you to exploit and can lead to opportunity.

Take yourself back to around 1870 and imagine what is happening on and off the field of play of a cricket match, somewhere in Glasgow, a city that is essentially the second most important place on the planet. Imagine who you are meeting, what the topics of conversation are about, what snippets of information you are hearing, what the viewpoints are about socio, economic and political matters, on trade and commerce, industry, colonialism, British expansionism, the Irish question, religion, temperance, education, invention and innovation. Visualise the atmosphere, the settings, the landscape, the people, the sights and smells, the differing opinions of class and privilege all thrown together into the level playing field of a game of cricket. The reliance upon others to be a part of something that brings about communication, participation and engagement for all involved.

This is egalitarianism in a scale that has never been considered, or even appreciated, and its affect on what we now take for granted, or expected, in the 21st Century, is certainly profound.

Of course, it is only a game of cricket, but as result of its own quirkiness that is missing from all other sports, it produces associations that are far more reaching than one would normally consider or even realise. That was Glasgow's secret with its "Big House" cricket. It had produced a market place for the exchange of ideas and a sharing of resources and expertise that shaped a United Kingdom.

You can draw your own conclusions and dismiss the suggestion out of hand, but ask yourself this before you do so: what would have happened without these Glasgow cricket clubs, their patrons, their members and their grounds? How different would society be today without considering what may or may not have happened in a cricket pavilion somewhere in the Glasgow area 140 odd years ago?

"The real price of every thing, what every thing really costs to the man who wants to acquire it, is the toil and trouble of acquiring it... But though labour be the real measure of the exchangeable value of all commodities, it is not that by which their value is commonly estimated... Every commodity, besides, is more frequently exchanged for, and thereby compared with, other commodities than with labour."

Adam Smith, The Wealth of Nations, 1776

WESTERN CRICKET CLUB.

Instituted 1862.

GROUND—GILMOREHILL PARK, SAUCHFIELD ROAD, HILLHEAD.

Patrons.—The Earl of Glasgow; Right Hon. H. A. Bruce, M.P., Home Secretary; Robert Dalglish, M.P.; John Laughland, &c. Vice-president, Jas. S. Hendry; secretary, J. G. Newlands, 22 Gladstone Street; treasurer, James Kelly, 18 George Square; captain, G. A. D. C. Fergusson; match secretary, Wm. C. Marshall, 38 Berkeley Terrace; directors, R. Wilson, jun., J. A. Mackay, C. M'Innes, A. Henderson, and A. Paterson, jun.; match committee, G. A. D. C. Fergusson, Wm. C. Marshall, and C. Fergusson.

Annual subscription, £1.

CLYDEGROVE CRICKET CLUB.

Instituted 1857.

GROUND—DIXON PARK, CALEDONIAN ROAD.

Patrons—W. S. Dixon, of Belleisle, R. Dalglish, M.P., W. Graham, M.P., Col. Buchanan, Drumpellier.

A. Cameron, president; A. Russell, 13 Clyde Terrace, secretary; Jas. M. Macreadie, 68 George Square, match secretary; J. Johnstone, treasurer; W. Stewart, J. Brownlie, and B. Burley, council. Members, 50.

BLYTHSWOOD CRICKET CLUB.

GROUND—QUEEN'S PARK, GREAT WESTERN ROAD.

Patrons.—Colonel Campbell of Blythswood; R. Dalglish, M.P.; Wm. Graham, M.P.; John Ramsay, Lord Dean of Guild.

G. S. Rogers, president; Richard Neilson, vice-president; A. M. Liddell, 63 Moray Place, West Cumberland Street, hon. secretary; A. B. M'Dougall, hon. treasurer; James Drake, recording secretary; James Liddell, jun., and M. M. Barry, match committee. General meetings of the club held on the first Wednesday of every month.

WEST-END CRICKET CLUB.
Established 1865.
Ground—Burnbank, Great Western Road.

Patrons—Robert Dalglish, Esq., Lieut-Colonel W. Holms, M.P., Alex. Whitelaw, Esq., M.P., Col. Buchanan, of Drumpellier; President, Alex. Porter, Esq.; Vice-president, Mr. R. M. Porter; Secretary, Mr. George Chirsey, 15 Windsor Street; Treasurer, Mr. James Jeffrey; Match Secretary, Mr. Daniel Foulner, 70 Renfrew Street. Annual subscription for Ordinary Members, 15s.; for Honorary Members, 10s.

GRANVILLE CRICKET CLUB.
GROUND—MYRTLE PARK, CROSSHILL.

Patrons—Right Hon. H. A. Bruce, M.P.; R. Dalglish, M.P.; Col. Buchanan, of Drumpellier; president, Wm. L. Rome; secretary, Wm. Ker; treasurer, Jas. Broadfoot. General Committee—R. Kinloch, W. H. Raeburn, A. Hosie, and W. E. Dick. Match Committee—A. Mackay, W. E. Dick, and Wm. Ross, secretary, 33 Apsley Place. Annual subscriptions for ordinary members, 21s.; honorary members, 10s. 6d.

SOUTHERN CRICKET CLUB.
GROUND—INGLEFIELD PARK, CATHCART ROAD.

The Right Hon. the Earl of Glasgow, Sir M. S. Stewart, Bart., R. Dalglish, M.P., Col. D. C. R. C. Buchanan of Drumpellier, patrons; J. Meikle, president; P. Fergus, captain; J. Brownlie, treasurer; J. W. Govan, 65 Jamaica Street, secretary.

General Meetings of the Club held on the First Tuesday of every month.

EAST-END CRICKET CLUB.
Instituted 1869.
GROUND—HELENVALE PARK, HIGH BELVIDERE.

Patrons—The Hon. the Lord Provost; Right Hon. the Earl of Glasgow; Dr. Chas. Cameron, M.P.; Alex. Whitelaw, M.P.; Bailie W. Collins; Councillor Finlay; Jas. A. Campbell, Esq.; John Matheson, jun., Esq.; Stephen Mason, Esq.; Daniel Burns, Esq.; president, John Mathie, M.D.; vice-president, James Wilson; secretary, Robert Farmer, 28 Tobago Street.

William and **James Baird** were the eldest and fourth of the eight sons and two daughters of Alexander Baird and Jean Moffat, from the Monklands area of Lanarkshire. The family moved from farming to coal mining and iron smelting, with the first Gartsherrie furnace opening in 1830. Alexander Baird, besides being a farmer, was also engaged in small scale coal working. In 1816 he leased from a Miss Alexander of Airdrie House, the coalfield of Rochsolloch, and it proved to be very successful. In 1822, the coal working became a bigger concern. Alexander secured the lease of the coalfield of Merryston on Newmains Farm that belonged to a Mr. Buchanan of Drumpellier House.

In 1826, Alexander leased the coalfields on the Gartsherrie Estate which resulted in pit after pit being sunk. Boats and plant were brought into requisition and The Canal Company constructed a branch to two of the pits. Arrangements were then made for delivering coal to Glasgow by canal or railway and when the Garnkirk and Glasgow Railway line opened in 1830, Baird had established the Gartsherrie Collieries as the most accessible in the country. By 1841, the purchase of leases of coal and iron rich land increased to such an extent that there were over 60 blast furnace sites and 37 coal pits operating. The impact of this explosion of industry saw the local population increase by over 30,000 in six short years.

The Baird family's relentless quest for coal and iron saw William Baird & Company turn their attention to the mineral rich lands of Ayrshire. In 1844, after negotiation with Lord Eglinton, the Eglinton Iron Works were established. Over time, James Baird would assume command of the Ayrshire operations and would add the Blair, Muirkirk, Lugar and Portland Iron Works to the company's ever expanding portfolio.

The Bairds also became directors in the Caledonian Railway Company who provided the majority of the rail infrastructure whether by shunting coal, transporting goods and materials such as the sandstone to build Glasgow or conveying the growing passenger use from A to B.

At the company's height in 1883, it was responsible for over 40 individual ironworks out of a Scottish total of 148. The consumption of coal at these 40 furnaces amounted to over 1,500 tons a day and all supplied by William Baird & Company collieries. The company employed over 10,000 men and boys and had a collective responsibility to a family population of around 40,000 people. In addition to all of this, the William Baird & Company had considerable influence in the development of the different railways such as the Glasgow, Cathcart, Bothwell, Hamilton, and Coatbridge railways, all authorised by an Act of Parliament in 1874 and all developed by the

Caledonian Railway Company.

The actual scale of the William Baird & Company operation is staggering to comprehend, let alone understand, and appreciate what was put in place for its workforce, the families and the local communities. By 1872, they had introduced compulsory religious instruction for all men within their employ and provided schooling and education for nearly 5,000 of their children. The erection of over 200 churches was funded by the company with the aim of *"the mitigation of spiritual destitution among the population of Scotland, through efforts for securing the godly upbringing of the young and the work of carrying the Gospel to the homes and hearts of all"*.

William Baird took over the business after his father's death in 1833, and served as the Unionist MP for the Falkirk Burghs 1841-46. He was a director of the Caledonian Railway Company and the Forth and Clyde Canal.

James Baird was the Unionist MP for the Falkirk Burghs 1850-57.

Jane Baird, youngest daughter of Alexander Baird, was born in 1804. She married a Mr. Thomas Jackson of Coats, the company that became J & P Coats of Ferguslie. J&P Coats amalgamated with Clark & Company Ltd in 1896 whose mills were at Anchor and Seedhill in Paisley.

Another creator of the establishment of cricket in Glasgow was a **Robert Dalglish**. His father, also Robert Dalglish, had been Lord Provost of Glasgow at the time of the first Reform Bill in 1832.

Robert (junior) was educated at Glasgow University and joined the family calico printing firm of R. Dalglish, Falconer & Co. He stood as an Independent Radical Member of Parliament for Glasgow in 1857, and his popularity was such that he was re-elected in 1859, 1865 and 1868 before retiring in 1874.

As an Independent Radical, a political party that eventually merged with the Whig party to form the Liberal party, he was involved in the bringing about of The Representation of the People Act 1867, also known as the Reform Act of 1867 or the Second Reform Act, and its Scottish counterpart, The Representation of the People (Scotland) Act 1868, important pieces of legislation that led to enfranchisement of the urban male working class throughout the United Kingdom.

Before the Act, only one million of the 5 million males in the United Kingdom were eligible to vote, and the passing of this Act instantly doubled the number of voters and at the same time, created a more equal distribution of electoral districts and delivered an increased measure of education. These reforms went on to change the face of British politics forever, and were important aspects that re-affirmed the conversion of Britain from being an agricultural nation to that of an industrialised nation with an ever-growing population.

Dalglish's patronage of various Glasgow cricket clubs allowed association football to capture the public imagination. The Western, Clydegrove, Blythswood, West End, Granville, West of Scotland, Kilmardinny, Southern and Alexandra cricket clubs all shared his patronage at some time, yet by 1890, only West of Scotland Cricket Club remained extant.

What is important to acknowledge though, is that four of these cricket clubs were responsible for the creation of the Scottish Football Association and the Scottish Cup in 1873.

Interestingly, West of Scotland Cricket Club remained at Hamilton Crescent, whereas the other clubs all moved location to meet the demands of Glasgow's increasing industrial and urban expansion.

Alexander Whitelaw was born at Drumpark in Monklands, the son of Janet Baird, the eldest of the family known as the "Bairds of Gartsherrie." He studied mining before entering the Gartsherrie Ironworks at the age of 18, where he soon became manager. In 1852 he was made a partner of the Eglinton Iron Company, and by 1860 had become a partner in the family firm of William Baird & Company.

He took a considerable interest in education, as the family firm maintained schools for the children of its 10,000-strong workforce. In 1873, when the Education Act came into law, he became a member of the first School Board of Glasgow and greatly improved the city's schooling system by securing sites for 15 new schools. He was elected to parliament in 1874, sitting as a Unionist, but overwork led to his early death, aged 56, on 1st July 1879.

Sir Charles Cameron was the son of John Cameron, a respected newspaper proprietor of Glasgow and Dublin. Educated at Madras Medical College, St Andrew's, and at Trinity College in Dublin, he also studied at medical schools in Paris, Berlin, and Vienna, but never went on to practice medicine.

He became editor of the North British Daily Mail in 1864 and then proprietor from 1873. He promoted both cricket and football by the simple inclusion of detailed scorecards and match reports that began to appear in the press.

In the 1874 General Election, Cameron was elected as a Liberal MP for Glasgow. His constituency was subsequently broken up as a result of the Redistribution of Seats Act 1885, but he was returned as the MP for the newly created Glasgow College constituency in the 1885 General Election which he held until 1895.

Cameron was created Baronet Cameron of Balclutha in 1893 in respect of his journalistic and parliamentary services. He returned to Westminster as the MP for Glasgow Bridgeton by way of a by-election in February 1897 until standing down at the 1900 General Election.

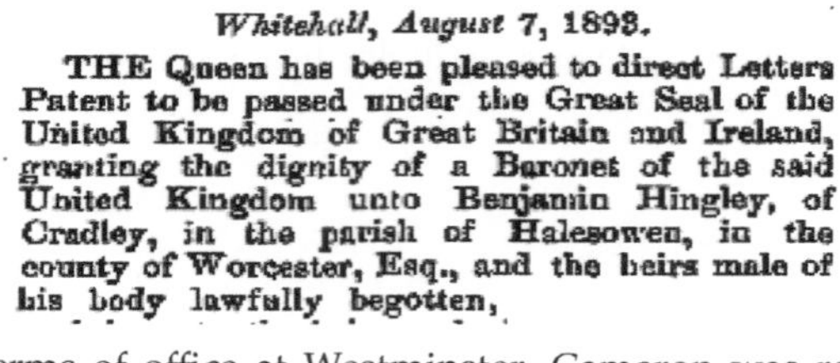

Whitehall, August 7, 1893.

THE Queen has been pleased to direct Letters Patent to be passed under the Great Seal of the United Kingdom of Great Britain and Ireland, granting the dignity of a Baronet of the said United Kingdom unto Benjamin Hingley, of Cradley, in the parish of Halesowen, in the county of Worcester, Esq., and the heirs male of his body lawfully begotten,

During his terms of office at Westminster, Cameron was responsible for the Inebriates Acts, secured various reforms in the Scottish Liquor Laws and was a member of the Royal Commission on the Liquor Licensing Laws in 1895. He was also behind laws conferring the municipal franchise on women, and acts abolishing imprisonment for debt in Scotland.

He was a member of the Departmental Committee on Habitual Offenders (Scotland) in 1894 and he also wrote a number of articles on medical, social, and political subjects.

A really important contributor to Glasgow's explosion as a city of renown is the **Dixon** family. William Dixon, originally a Northumberland miner, was the owner of the Govan coalfields. He purchased the Calder Ironworks in Coatbridge and exploited the nearby Monkland coalfields. Such was the development of his business, he went on to purchase the neighbouring Palacecraig Estate in Coatbridge and the Faskine Estate in Airdrie.

The quest for coal and iron became so demanding, Dixons, the company, subsequently bought numerous estates in and around Glasgow such as Govanhill, Crosshill, Carfin, Broomelton, Larkhall, Earnockmuir, Blantyre and Mosesfield along with properties at Wilsontown, Garturk and Fauldhouse and established collieries, blast furnaces and malleable ironworks.

His son, also William Dixon, founded the Govan Ironworks in 1837 for the manufacture of bar iron, the production of iron castings for steam-engines and general engineering products. These works became known as 'Dixon Blazes' as the light from the furnaces illuminated the night sky on the south side of Glasgow. He further expanded the colliery side of the business through short-term lease of fields owned by the Stirling Maxwell estates and added new mines at such places as Cockerhill, Titwood, and Ibrox.

When the Clyde Trustees would not carry his coal and iron at acceptable rates, William Dixon simply built a railway, called the Polloc and Govan Railway, and Dixon's coal and iron products were carried to Greenock by rail. Although the name of the surrounding area that gave its name to the railway company is called Pollok and close by is called Pollokshields, the Act of Parliament authorising the railway used the spelling Polloc. It was authorised in 1830 and it linked Govan with the River Clyde at the Broomielaw, the Glasgow, Paisley and Johnstone Canal and also Rutherglen and opened in 1840 and was bought by the Clydesdale Junction Railway Company in 1846. Later in the same year, The General Terminus and Glasgow Harbour Railway was authorised and subsequently opened in 1848. Its main function was intended to be the transportation of coal from collieries in Lanarkshire and Ayrshire over other railways, to a centralised coal depot on the south bank of the River Clyde. This unification of the various railways linked the Polloc and Govan Railway with the Glasgow and Paisley Joint Railway, the Glasgow, Paisley, Kilmarnock and Ayr Railway, the Glasgow, Barrhead and Kilmarnock Joint Railway and the Clydesdale Junction Railway, and collectively, they were all swallowed up in a purchase by the Caledonia Railway Company, who just so happened to have a certain William Dixon as the major shareholder.

The various Dixon companies were nationalised under the 1951 Iron and

Steel Act and became part of the Iron and Steel Corporation of Great Britain and by 1954, Dixon's Ironworks were transferred to Colvilles by the Holding and Realization Agency in order to allow rationalisation of the Scottish steel industry.

The former estates of Govanhill and Crosshill were mined for coal and iron, and when these were exhausted by the 1860s, urban regeneration took over. Housing in streets named as Calder Street, Garturk Street, Carfin Street, Dixon Avenue and Dixon Road appeared, along with others named after Dixon's daughters such as Allison Street, Daisy Street and Annette Street. Public libraries, churches, schools, baths, shops etc were provided and parks were created such as Dixon Park and Myrtle Park, and within these, many cricket clubs sprang up, Clydegrove, Lancelot, Kilmardinny, Third Lanark, Southern, Alexandra and Granville to name but seven. Most were lost by 1890, but their original existences have significant importance to what would transpire in the establishment of football as the "people's sport".

QUEEN'S PARK. - This beautiful park of eighty acres, once known as Pathhead Farm, was named after the monarch whose hopes of remaining Queen of Scots were forever shattered at the battle of Langside. Although known by this name, it is supposed the battlefield extended to the ground where the memorial monument of the conflict is erected. Acquired in 1857 at a cost of £30,000, with the object of opening up for building the southern outskirts of the city, the years 1858-59 were occupied with laying it out, draining, etc.

The amount of money expended on these purposes was estimated at about other £30,000, and a number of the unemployed found something to do in the work of preparing the park for the opening day on 11th September, 1862. "The Queen's" is well wooded - ash, beech, birch, chestnut, elm, and plane trees being found in it, while the rhododendron and holly are seen everywhere. The air is melodious with the songs of birds, and the somewhat discordant "caw-caw" of the crows falls on the ear - a small rookery of these blackcoats being in the neighbourhood.

In the park are two arbours, several rustic vases, seats in shady walks, a flower terrace 750 feet long by 140 feet wide, reached from the lower ground by a granite stair, football and cricket fields, bowling greens, lawn tennis courts, and, as advertisers sometimes say, "other attractions too numerous to mention."

Like the forgotten lands of ancient Mesopotamia, it being the cradle of western civilisation, the industrial development and following urbanisation of areas of Glasgow, such as Govanhill, Crosshill and Queen's Park would be responsible for the birth and development of a new belief, and this new belief was association football.

The Gallant Pioneers of the Beautiful Game

Queen's Park

Queen's Park are not just Scotland's oldest football association club, they are the football association club that influenced the initial development of the sport in Scotland, continued throughout Britain and then took the game to the world. The majority of the concepts that we enjoy with association football played all around the world in the 21st Century, such as cross-bars, the offside rule, free kicks, throw-ins, the duration of matches and most of the rules, all evolved from the efforts of the early members of Queen's Park Football Club and their mission to create another form of recreational sport for all to enjoy. Initially drawn from the prosperous upper and middle classes of Glasgow, their style of football and traditions inspired the working classes and artisans to flock to the sport.

With what had originally started as a number of young men kicking a football around in a public park for their mutual recreation and amusement and their zest for the new sport of "football" that was emerging in England at the time, these same young men discussed the possibility of organising themselves into a club for like-minded individuals. If they had enough people interested in forming and operating a club similar to the extant Glasgow cricket clubs all around them, why not just simply create a club of their own, a football club, especially when there were no other football clubs in Scotland? Someone has to create a point of origin, so why not them?

A meeting was called and took place within No.3 Eglinton Terrace, Victoria Road, Glasgow on Tuesday 9th July 1867.

The original minutes state:

To-night, at half-past eight o'clock, a number of gentlemen met at No. 3 Eglinton Terrace for the purpose of forming a "football club."

After Mr. Black was called to the chair, a good deal of debating ensued, and ultimately the following measures were voted for and carried, viz.:—

First. That the club should be called the "Queen's Park Football Club."

Second. That there should be four office-bearers, viz.:—A president, captain, secretary, and treasurer.

Third. That there should be thirteen members of committee, including office-bearers, seven of whom to form a quorum. "

The following gentlemen were then duly elected as office-bearers and members of committee, viz.:—

1.	Mr.	Ritchie, president.	
2.	,,	Black, captain.	
3.	,,	Klinger, secretary.	
4.	,,	Smith, sen., treasurer.	
5.	,,	Grant, member of committee.	
6.	,,	Gardner, sen.,	,,
7.	,,	R. Davidson,	,,
8.	,,	Smith, jun.,	,,
9.	,,	Edmiston,	,,
10.	,,	P. Davidson,	,,
11.	,,	Gladstone,	,,
12.	,,	Reid,	,,
13.	,,	Skinner,	,,

With having founded the Queen's Park Football Club, the newly-appointed office bearers embarked upon the mission to establish a code of rules for the future playing of the game to follow and for newly created football clubs to adopt.

Queen's Park held their first committee meeting on 9th August 1867, again the venue was No.3 Eglinton Terrace, Victoria Road, Glasgow. At this meeting at which ten committee members were present, the first constitution of the Queen's Park Football Club was drawn up and the club also adopted the "Rules of the Field," kindly provided by Mr. James Lillywhite, the famous Nottinghamshire cricketer whose family also operated the renowned tobacconist and sports outfitter business in London.

The minutes from this second meeting state:

First—That this club shall be called the "Queen's Park Football Club," and its object shall be, the recreation and amusement of its members.

Second.—That the office-bearers shall consist of a president, captain, secretary, and treasurer, to be elected annually by ballot; retiring office-bearers eligible for re-election.

Third.—That there be a committee of thirteen members, including office-bearers, seven of whom to form a quorum at each meeting.

Fourth.—That the secretary shall have power at any time to call a meeting of committee for special purposes.

Fifth.—That the committee meet once a month, from April to October inclusive, and once during the winter months.

Sixth.—That applicants for membership, on being proposed and seconded, shall be admitted, provided that a majority of the committee agree.

Seventh.— That each party pay a shilling of entry money on being admitted into membership.

Eighth.—That the expenses of the club shall be defrayed by an annual subscription of sixpence, payable in June.

At this meeting, the "Rules on the Field" provided by James Lillywhite were discussed, revised and then adopted. This same James Lillywhite had been employed as the professional cricketer for Clydesdale Cricket Club in the 1850s. These rules were originally those of the English Football Association who themselves had taken the then basic rules of the game, as originally designed by Cambridge University, modified and then codified them in 1863. The alterations made to these rules by Queen's Park Football Club is probably the historical turning point in the establishment of association football, the resultant effect of the playing of the game in Scotland and England and beyond as well as being the beginning of the separation between the association football and rugby football codes that, until this point, had enjoyed "crossover" elements in the rules and playing of both sports.

It might be viewed as being typically Glaswegian obdurate defiance to change the accepted "Rules of the Field", but these actions of the Queen's Park Football Club office bearers are based on the principles of equality and fairness to all participating. The club's own motto, *Ludere Causa Ludendi* - "to play for the sake of playing" exemplifies the ambience of fairness that the club has always projected and maintained since foundation, and is also extremely similar to the "Spirit of the Game" ethics that cricketers are bound to observe.

The infant Queens' Park, having formed as a club and then established rules to play to and abide by, now faced the problem of who to actually play against. Queen's Park actively sought out other clubs, or similar groups of men to themselves who could be garnered into forming a football club in terms of the template that they had created.

A handful of clubs were sourced, their founding being after Queen's Park, and were challenged to games. Queen's Park Football Club actively encouraged other clubs to participate under recognised rules and organisation akin to the constitutional requirements that they had created for their own club.

Queen's Park had played in the initial English Football Association Cup competition in March 1872, and had met the Wanderers at The Oval, the home of Surrey County Cricket Club, on the 4th March. The match itself ended 0-0 but Queen's Park could not afford a return trip to London for the replay and the Wanderers progressed to the final. But the club still faced difficulty procuring Scottish opposition and in the 1871-72 season, had only played three other games. Since formation, their early games were infrequent and involved cricket clubs such as Airdrie and Hamilton, and near neighbours Thistle, Granville and Southern. They had challenged clubs such as Glasgow Academical Rugby Club who politely declined citing the difference in the codes.

But all was about to change...

In late May 1872, Queen's Park had written to a number of Scottish rugby and association football clubs in attempts to arrange fixtures but without success, however, Queen's Park had now established that there were definitely other association rules playing football clubs in existence. They were further bolstered in their endeavours when they discovered that most of them were cricket clubs whose memberships were turning to association football as a means of keeping fit during the winter months. With these possible opponents being cricket clubs, it meant that Queen's Park now had access to a number of organised clubs that met the desires of what Queen's Park wanted, and that was the provision of regular opposition, and these clubs were Vale of Leven, Dumbarton, Renton, Clydesdale, 3rd L.R.V, Kilmarnock and Airdrie, and all were in reasonable travelling distance.

At the same time, Queen's Park wrote to Charles W. Alcock, Hon. Secretary of the Football Association in London to ascertain what arrangements had been made in respect of the playing of an international match in Scotland. On 28th September 1872, Mr. Alcock replied that the Football Association would send an England team to Glasgow to play a Scotland team in late November, but would be dependent on what facilities, railway or otherwise, would be afforded to the visiting team.

The committee of Queen's Park Football Club seized upon this chance to finally popularise the game north of the border and unanimously accepted the challenge of arranging the match. Accommodation was arranged and a post-match dinner would be provided to the English team in the Carrick Hotel. The promotion of the match and the various arrangements for staging it had all been attended to, and although Glasgow Academical Rugby Club had kindly offered their ground at Burnbank for the hosting of this international, Hamilton Crescent, the ground of West of Scotland Cricket Club in Partick, was the preferred venue.

When the first official international match between England and Scotland took place at West of Scotland's cricket ground at Hamilton Crescent on Saturday 30th November 1872, the entire Scotland team was comprised of players from Queen's Park Football Club.

The Queen's Park players turned out in their club kit of navy and white. This combination has remained the national team's first choice colours to this day.

QUEEN'S PARK

INTERNATIONAL
FOOT-BALL MATCH
SCOTLAND
VERSUS
ENGLAND
ASSOCIATION RULES
WEST OF SCOTLAND
CRICKET GROUND
HAMILTON CRESCENT, PARTICK
SATURDAY, 30th NOVEMBER, 1872
2.00PM
ADMISSION - ONE SHILLING

INTERNATIONAL
FOOT-BALL MATCH,
(Association Rules.)
ENGLAND v. SCOTLAND,
WEST OF SCOTLAND CRICKET GROUND,
Hamilton Crescent, Partick,
SATURDAY, 30th November, 1872, at 2 p.m.
ADMISSION-ONE SHILLING.

SCOTLAND: (2-2-6)

Robert W. Gardner (c)

William Ker, Joseph Taylor

James Thomson, James Smith

Robert Smith, Robert Leckie, Alexander Rhind, Billy MacKinnon, Jerry Weir, David Wotherspoon

ENGLAND: (1-1-8)

Robert Barker (Hertfordshire Rangers)

Ernest Greenhalgh (Notts County)

Reginald de Courtenay Welch (Harrow Chequers)

Frederick Chappell (Oxford University), William Maynard (1st Surrey Rifles), John Brockbank (Cambridge University), Charles Clegg (Sheffield Wednesday), Arnold Kirke-Smith (Oxford University), Cuthbert Ottaway (Oxford University) (c), Charles Chenery (Crystal Palace), Charles Morice (Barnes)

The first ever case for goal line technology occurred during this game when Scotland had a goal disallowed in the first half after the umpires decided that the ball had not cleared the tape.

Remember – this was played in the days before crossbars let alone nets!

Despite a combined presence of 14 attacking players and only 3 defenders, the game ended 0-0.

It would be another 98 years before the two sides would produce a goalless draw.

Although the game itself was a goalless draw, it is regarded as the first International football match, and more importantly, in respect of the significance to Scottish sporting history, it was played on a cricket ground in Glasgow. The further impact that the Glasgow area cricket clubs had upon the early development of association football was about to take a huge step forward.

In the space of a year, Queen's Park Football Club had made history by playing against the Wanderers at The Oval in London, the home of Surrey County Cricket Club, in the semi-final of the inaugural English Football Association Cup. A few months later, Queen's Park had gone on to become a rising sporting power in the land as well as becoming an international example for all to admire.

When the players, the majority of whom were employed in offices, stores and warehouses, had turned out as a Scotland team against England in the first international, they had become legends in the Scottish conscientious.

This story of a solitary club representing a country that stood against the might of a nation, gave association football the impetus it so desperately required. Within months, the number of clubs increased and Queen's Park were no longer in isolation.

Everyone wanted to play them.

Queen's Park, on the back of the rising interest in this new sport, quickly realised that it should form an association for all the emergent clubs to join. There was the Football Association in England so why not form a Scottish governing body with its own rules and regulations and involve the dozen or so clubs?

An advertisement was placed in a Glasgow newspaper in February 1873 asking for representatives of clubs to attend a meeting within the Dewar's Temperance Hotel, 11 Bridge Street, Glasgow on 13th March 1873, the purpose of which was to form an association to introduce a governance structure for the sport and its member clubs.

Seven clubs attended this convened meeting, namely Queen's Park, Clydesdale, Vale of Leven, Dumbreck, Third Lanark, Eastern and Granville with Kilmarnock sending a letter of interest to join. Apart from Queen's Park, the seven others were cricket clubs.

The meeting saw the election of office-bearers and the endorsement of the rules and regulations that Queen's Park had created as the template for all to follow.

These eight clubs have the honour of being the founding fathers of the Scottish Football Association.

Within a few short years, the number of clubs had gone into the hundreds and football had definitely caught the imagination of the Scottish people as the winter alternative to cricket as the national sport.

1873 saw Queen's Park Football Club, along with a large number of cricket clubs, become founder members of the Scottish Football Association and helped with the introduction of the inaugural Scottish Cup. 16 clubs embarked on the quest for the first Scottish Cup in October 1873. The original participating clubs were Alexandra Athletic, Blythswood, Callander, Clydesdale, Dumbarton, Dumbreck, Eastern, Granville, Kilmarnock, Queen's Park, Renton, Rovers, Southern, 3rd Lanark Rifle Volunteers, Vale of Leven and Western.

Queen's Park won the inaugural Scottish Cup without conceding a single goal, with victories over Dumbreck, Eastern and Renton culminating in a 2-0 win against Clydesdale in the final, which was played at Hampden Park in front of a crowd of 2,500.

Hampden Park was Queen's Park's home ground and it had been agreed previously that the final would be played there as Queen's Park had contributed significantly to the cost of the trophy that they eventually won.

Queen's Park's preparation, training and experimentation with tactics and styles of play became their signature, but they maintained a strict amateur code. They still remain the only amateur club playing senior league and cup football in the world.

Within the context of the emergence of association football in Scotland, the late historian and broadcaster Bob Crampsey compared the role of the Queen's Park club with that of the MCC in cricket and the R&A Club in golf.

Queen's Park's diligence in providing the early playing rules in Scotland, their early management of the Scotland national team and the introduction of the Scottish Football Association and Scottish Football Association Challenge Cup provide more than ample evidence to confirm their status as the "Premier" club of Scotland.

Queens' Park's home Hampden was originally a cricket ground, complete with a pavilion. When the cricket pavilion at Hampden was replaced in 1878, Queen's Park purchased, at a cost of £65, the Caledonian Cricket Club's pavilion at Kelvinbridge, which was then taken down and reconstructed at Hampden at a cost of £84.

This same pavilion was then later sold on to Hampden Bowling Club and still forms the centre part of the current bowling clubhouse.

By the mid-1880s, Queen's Park regularly drew 10,000 spectators for friendly matches and when they left their original Hampden Park ground, the UK's first enclosed football stadium with turnstiles, for a new purpose-built stadium near Crosshill in 1884, the Hampden Park name was retained.

This ground was later sold to Third Lanark and renamed Cathkin Park.

Granville

Granville Cricket Club played at Myrtle Park in Crosshill, Glasgow. Their ground was adjacent to Queen's Park Football Club's original Hampden ground. The background to the founding of Granville Cricket Club is utterly fascinating and goes some way to explain the many political, socio and cultural changes that were happening in Glasgow at the height of the Industrial Revolution.

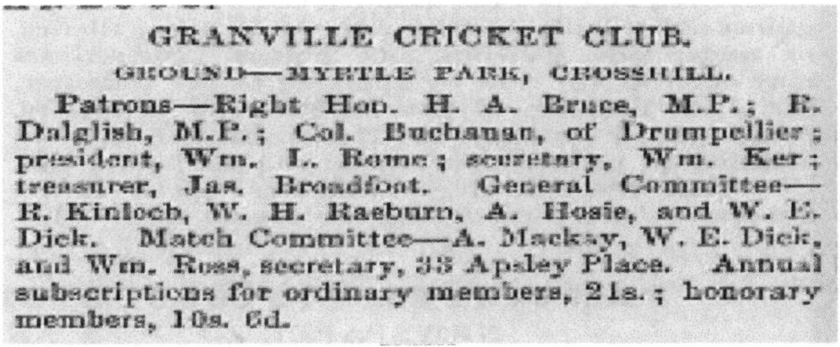

GRANVILLE CRICKET CLUB.

GROUND—MYRTLE PARK, CROSSHILL.

Patrons—Right Hon. H. A. Bruce, M.P.; R. Dalglish, M.P.; Col. Buchanan, of Drumpellier; president, Wm. L. Rome; secretary, Wm. Ker; treasurer, Jas. Broadfoot. General Committee—R. Kinloch, W. H. Raeburn, A. Hosie, and W. E. Dick. Match Committee—A. Mackay, W. E. Dick, and Wm. Ross, secretary, 33 Apsley Place. Annual subscriptions for ordinary members, 21s.; honorary members, 10s. 6d.

The cricket club was another supported venture of Colonel Buchanan of Drumpellier, but its principal patron and founder was a Welshman called Henry Bruce. Henry Bruce came from Duffryn, Aberdare, Glamorganshire, whose family had received great wealth as a result of the discovery of coal on the estates of Duffryn and Aberdare. From 1847 to 1854, Bruce was the stipendiary magistrate for Merthyr Tydfil and Aberdare, but resigned the position when he was elected as the Liberal Member of Parliament for Merthyr Tydfil.

He became involved in the management of the Dowlais Iron Company, and in 1862, he was made Under-Secretary of State for the Home Department. However, he lost his seat in 1868 but managed to be re-elected to parliament via the vacant seat for Renfrewshire whereupon, the Prime Minister, William Gladstone, made him Home Secretary. Bruce's reign as Home Secretary saw him introduce a reform of the licensing laws, and he was responsible for the Licensing Act 1872, which made the magistrates the licensing authority, increased the penalties for misconduct in public-houses and shortened the number of hours for the sale of alcohol.

His other important contributions were the introduction of compulsory colliery schools where the children of the mining work-force received an education. He was raised to the peerage in 1873 to become Lord Aberdare.

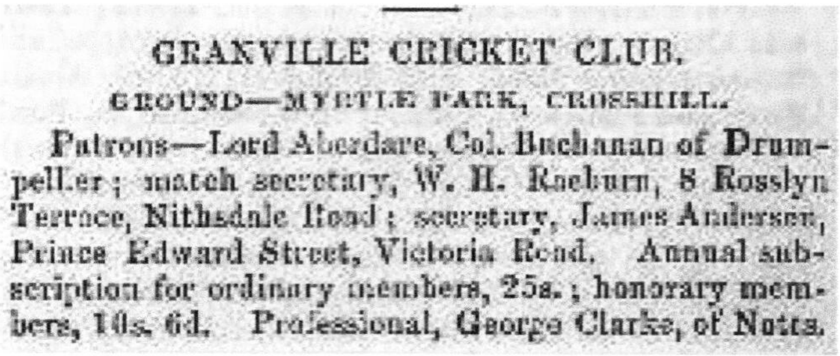

GRANVILLE CRICKET CLUB.

GROUND—MYRTLE PARK, CROSSHILL.

Patrons—Lord Aberdare, Col. Buchanan of Drumpellier; match secretary, W. H. Raeburn, 8 Rosslyn Terrace, Nithsdale Road; secretary, James Anderson, Prince Edward Street, Victoria Road. Annual subscription for ordinary members, 25s.; honorary members, 10s. 6d. Professional, George Clarke, of Notts.

One of the many interests that Henry Bruce was involved in was the Historical Society for Great Britain. It originally operated as a type of gentlemen's club where facts, figures, historical data and matters of interest were collated and shared among the members, but also preserved for the nation to enjoy. In 1868, after a campaign led by Henry Bruce that brought this society to a larger public and that its work was of national importance, Queen Victoria granted a 'Royal' charter and the society is now known as the Royal Historical Society.

The Royal Historical Society promotes historical research nationally and supports and represents those engaged professionally in researching and presenting public history that can be found in libraries, museums, archives and the heritage industry. Recognition of the importance of the Royal Historical Society's role within the public domain can be seen with its involvement in many government initiatives and various projects with national institutions such as the British Library and the National Archives.

Henry Bruce had seven daughters and two sons, and the cricket club was named after the youngest son, Charles Granville Bruce, whose middle name was in homage to Earl Granville, the popular leader of the Liberal Party in the House of Lords. This son would go on to become Brigadier-General Charles Granville Bruce, the famous Himalayan mountaineering veteran and leader of the second and third British expeditions to try and conquer Mount Everest in 1922 and 1924.

This Bruce, who had earned the reputation of being a hard-drinking, larger than life character, simply referred to himself as 'Charlie' and his peers called him "Bruiser". He had served a swashbuckling career with the Gurkhas (1889–1920) and had been severely wounded at Gallipoli in World War I.

Bruce was determined to conquer Mount Everest, and the 1924 trip saw the disappearance of George Mallory and Andrew Irvine on their summit attempt. It is still an argument whether both men reached the summit but we will never know if they succeeded in completing Bruce's goal of having an expedition conquer Everest.

Granville Cricket Club formed an association football team in 1872 and was one of the original founders of the Scottish Football Association. The club also played as one of the sixteen teams that participated in the first Scottish Cup competition. Unfortunately Granville suffered defeat in the first round of the 1873-74 season, losing 6-0 to eventual finalists Clydesdale and the team did not participate in future years.

Clydesdale v Granville

This match which is now about the last of the football fixtures in the district, was played on the fine ground of the Clydesdale, Kinning Park, on Saturday, and, after a hotly contested game, resulted in a draw. The dribbling of Broadfoot, Ker, and Kinloch, for the Granville, and that of McPherson, M'Arley, and Taylor for the Clydesdale, was really good. The Clydesdale had the best of the first half of the game, and pressed their opponents pretty tightly till near the close, several tough scrimmages occurring near the Granville goal line, where several shots were tried, but without effect, the stronghold being ably guarded by Ker, who resisted all attempts. Several fine short runs were made by Broadfoot, Keay, and Kinloch, who got the ball well up to the Clydesdale fortress, but the steady play of Campbell, Swan, and W. Wilson did not allow it to remain there long. In the second half, however, the Clydesdale had just sufficient work cut out for them, and, had it not been for the goal-keeper, who did his duty well, several well directed attempts to get the ball under (one by Ker and another by Broadfoot) would undoubtedly have been successful. The Clydesdale were deprived of two of their best players - Messrs Gibb and Hendry. The following are the respective teams:-Clydesdale - McNab (goal), W. Wilson and A. Sinclair (backs), A. Campbell and J. Swan (half backs), A. Taylor, Anderson, M'Pherson, M'Arley, J. Wilson, and G. Webster (forwards). Granville - W. Ker (goal), Neil, Hetherington (backs), Raeburn (captain), MacKay (half-backs), Kinloch (fly kick), Broadfoot, Rae, Kaey, Malcolm, and Lyon (forwards).

Granville's main claim to fame, however, is for contributing three players for the Scotland team in the first ever international football match in 1872, though all players officially played for Queen's Park. Captain Robert W. Gardner, William Ker, and James Thomson played against England in the 0-0 draw at Hamilton Crescent.

The club folded in 1878.

As an addendum to the Granville story and the sporting and historical legacies that it was indirectly responsible for, it would be remiss of me not to mention the exploits of Henry Bruce's grandson, Clarence Napier Bruce, the 3rd Baron Aberdare.

Clarence Napier Bruce was a keen sportsman who won the British, French and US amateur tennis titles, qualified for the Open golf championship, and played 96 first-class cricket matches for Middlesex from 1908 until 1929 and scored 4,316 runs at an average 28.96. Against Lancashire at Lord's in 1919, he hit 149 and in 1921, scored 144 against Warwickshire.

GRANVILLE

His enthusiasm for sport was fanatical. This was a man that truly understood that the health and well-being of a nation could be improved by recreation and was adamant that all classes should be encouraged to participate in sport and that there should be greater accessibility for all classes to enjoy the experience of playing sport.

In the aftermath of the horrors of the Great War, he argued that the loss of one generation, through conflict, had been replaced with another that was, in his opinion, generally undernourished and mainly employed in sedentary jobs thus leaving Britain poorly equipped to remain, let alone maintain, its standing as an economic or military power.

He railed against the sporting establishment who were opposed to sending a GB team to the 1928 Olympics in Amsterdam citing the burden of cost was prohibitive and that participation may not be in the national interest.

Undeterred by this opposition, in 1927, Bruce simply used his own sporting profile to raise funds, and his actions were a radical departure from normal practice, as up to that point in time, the selection of athletes to represent Great Britain had been elitist and determined from only those who could finance themselves to participate.

He urged patrons and friends to *"Become missionaries and go out into athletic circles in which you move, to spread the gospel of the Olympic ideal, so that we might equip, transport and house the British teams selected to go to Amsterdam."* and this enthusiasm subsequently raised £40,000, the equivalent of a million pounds today.

The Amsterdam Olympics saw Britain send 232 competitors, 201 men and 31 women, who took part in 84 events in 14 different sports with Team GB finishing in 11th place in the final medal table.

In 1937, with the storm clouds of yet another European conflict gathering, the government appointed Bruce as the Chairman of the National Fitness Council.

The drive and determination of Bruce was instrumental in the bringing of the 1948 Olympics to a war-torn London, when the opinion of the general public, fuelled by vehement criticism in the national press, demanded cancellation as in 1940 and 1944.

Dubbed the "Austerity Olympics", Bruce was determined to prove that sport would help heal Britain and the world. He had come from a generation of military officers that were used to making executive decisions and getting things done, and having been given a budget of only £750,000.00 to deliver the Games, he proved all his critics and doubters wrong with the hosting of a success that also returned a £29,000.00 profit.

Bruce relentlessly championed sport and was also an ardent campaigner for the National Playing Fields Association until his death in 1957 at the age of 72.

The Olympic ideal and the pursuit of a promise was finally realised in May 2012 when British climber, Kenton Cool, successfully carried an Olympic gold medal to the top of Mount Everest. Kenton Cool, 38, from Gloucestershire, while also breaking his own British record with his tenth ascent, took with him a medal from the 1924 Winter Olympics, and in doing so, fulfilled a pledge made by a member of the 1922 British Everest expedition. Cool had been loaned one of the medals awarded to the team by Charles Wakefield, the grandson of Dr Arthur Wakefield, a member of the 1922 expedition led by Brigadier-General Charles Granville Bruce and Lt Col Edward Strutt, who provided medical care to his comrades, including George Mallory and Andrew Irvine.

With the 1924 Winter Olympics in France, 13 members of the 1922 expedition – 12 British and one Australian – were honoured with medals for mountaineering. Lt Col Edward Strutt, who accepted the medals, pledged to place one on the summit of Everest. But this promise was never kept.

Clydesdale

The story of Clydesdale Cricket Club, its founding, evolvement, good fortune, various patronages and its success as THE premier sports club in the Glasgow area, is one that is not readily evident to those outside of Scottish cricket circles.

It is quite sad to consider, and this is a personal opinion of course, that the majority of the population of Scotland is unaware of this club and that Clydesdale Cricket Club is deprived of the praise and recognition it so richly deserves to receive as probably being one of the country's most important sporting institutions. The landscape of much of Scotland's sporting history of the last 160 odd years would be very different if Clydesdale had not been involved along the way.

In fact, and I write this with no offence targeted at the club itself, the importance of the early Clydesdale story is not even appreciated, let alone known, by the majority of the membership of the club. The club has played key roles in the establishment of cricket, football, rugby and hockey as sports and past-times to be enjoyed by the people of Glasgow and also Scotland.

It has had internationalists in all four fields and is currently at the forefront of examples to be used as templates of "best working practice" in the engagement, encouragement and development of children in participation in Scotland's two biggest team sports after football, namely cricket and hockey.

Clydesdale's fortunes have ebbed and flowed over the years, but it has remained constant and consistent in what it delivers: access to all for participation in sport and recreation, irrespective of capability, to those that wish to do so. And it does so and will continue to do so.

Clydesdale Cricket Club had been founded in 1848 by an Archibald Campbell of Hawick. The club started off with an initial membership of 27 created by the merger of the Thistle and Wallace-grove Cricket Clubs into a single entity, Clydesdale. The first games played in 1848 by this new "merged" club, Clydesdale, were at a field in the Kinning Park area of Glasgow, on ground leased from a Mr. Tweedie, whose occupation has simply been described as a "cow feeder". This field had been previously used by the now defunct Wallace-grove Cricket Club.

CLYDESDALE CRICKET CLUB.
Instituted 1848.

GROUND—KINNING PARK, PAISLEY ROAD.

The Earl of Eglinton and Winton, patron; Robert Arthur, president; Robert Drysdale, vice-president; John Cumming, Charles Cruickshanks, and William M'Comb, council; D. W. Connochie, William M'Comb, Kennedy Leck; Archibald Campbell, and R. F. Graham, match committee; Thomas M'Arly, 1 Stanley Place, Paisley Road, hon. treasurer; R. F. Graham, 273 Sauchiehall St., hon. secretary. Annual subscription for ordinary members, £1 11s 6d; hon. members, £1 1s. The monthly meetings of the club are held on the first Thursday of each month.

MEMBERS.

Arthur, R.
Balgarnie, J.
Baird, A. S.
Bone, D. D.
Campbell, A.
Campbell, C.
Clarke, H.
Connochie, D. W.
Connochie, W.
Cruickshanks, C.
Cumming, J.
Drysdale, R.
Duff, D.
Duff, J.
Douglas, J. H.
Donald, G.
Grainger, J., jun.
Glen, A.
Gilchrist, J.
Gass, J.
Graham, R. F.
Hall, J.
Hendry, E.
Henry, J.
Jopson, D.
Laing, W. R. A.
Leck, K.
Luske, W.
Miller, J.
Morrison, J. M.
M'Arly, J.
M'Arly, T.
M'Donald, K.
Macdonald, S.
M'Comb, T.
M'Comb, W.
M'Ewan, W.
M'Allister, A.
M'Kinnon, J.
M'Gibbon, M. C.
M'Neil, J.
M'Pherson, W.
M'Lean, J.
Nimmo, J.
Orr, J., jun.
Stuart, J.
Swan, W.
M'Lurkin, J. B.
Wallace, J.
Walker, J., jun.
Walker, R. M.
Wood, W.
Wright, A. M.

Archie Campbell

In 1849, Clydesdale moved the short distance of 500 yards south-west to fields leased from a Mr Meiklewham, just west of the newly built General Terminus Railway in Kinning Park, and it was there that they remained until 1876.

I have often wondered how Clydesdale Cricket Club got its name, and given the fact that the club was the result of a merger between the Thistle and Wallace-grove Cricket Clubs, I am going to be bold to suggest that the new club's name was perhaps derived from a local source and reflective of events that were happening close by.

The General Terminus and Glasgow Harbour Railway had been commissioned in July 1846 and opened in December 1848. For its completion, land had been required to be given up by the owners.

The main purpose of the railway was to be for the transportation of coal from collieries in Lanarkshire and Ayrshire over other railways, to a coal depot on the south bank of the River Clyde.

This new railway linked the Polloc and Govan Railway with the Glasgow and Paisley Joint Railway, the Glasgow, Paisley, Kilmarnock and Ayr Railway and the Glasgow, Barrhead and Kilmarnock Joint Railway, however, there was a local line already in place and it was being used as the central point of convergence for the new General Terminus in Kinning Park, and this line was called the Clydesdale Junction Railway.

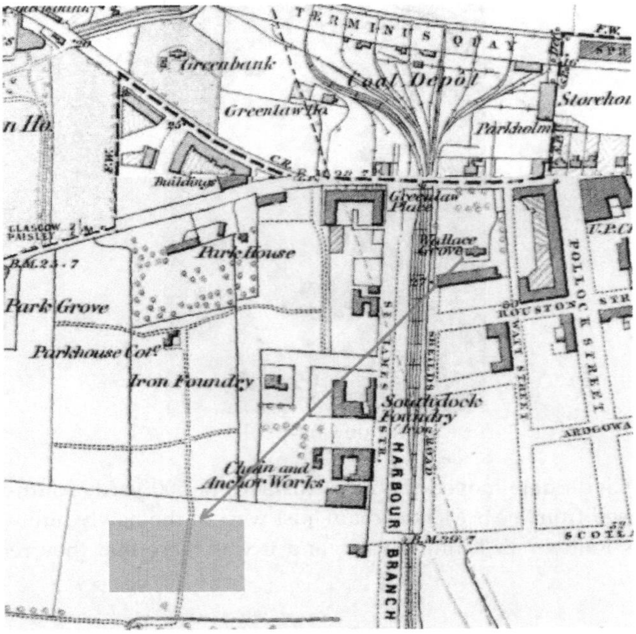

One of Clydesdale's early patrons, the Earl of Eglinton and Winton, was a financial beneficiary of the creation of The General Terminus and Harbour Railway in Kinning Park.

It is an anecdotal story, but according to legend, the members of the Wallacegrove Cricket Club, a young club whose members possessed an enthusiasm to become bigger and better, secured a new field in Kinning Park, and after convening a special meeting of the membership, changed the name of the club to reflect its new locale, "The Clydesdale".

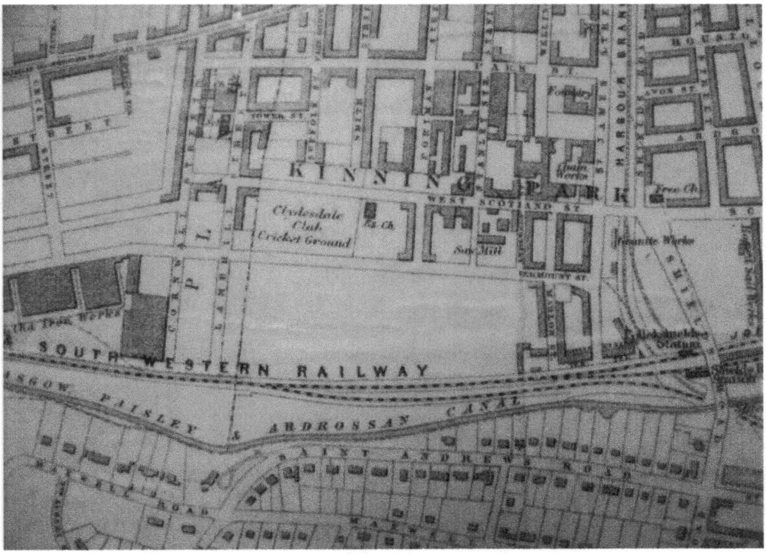

Archibald William Montgomerie, 13th Earl of Eglinton, having taken up the game at Eton, became an active member of Clydesdale Cricket Club whose Kinning Park ground would host invitational matches, including, in 1851, an England eleven.

In three short years, Clydesdale Cricket Club had become the epicentre of the promotion and development of cricket in the west of Scotland culminating with the holding of a number of invitational games at Kinning Park over the course of the following two decades.

In September 1851, Clydesdale's ground at Kinning Park became the venue for an exhibition match between the Twenty Two of Glasgow versus an All England Eleven. The match was played over three days on the 18th, 19th and 20th September.

Marquees and tents were erected all around the ground and companies and salesmen exhibited their wares for the good people of Glasgow to peruse. Fred Lillywhite, the proprietor of the famous "Lillywhite Brothers - Tobacconist and Sports Outfitter", in London was present, and his good friends, Jonny Wisden, George Parr and William Caffyn were playing for the All England Eleven. Wisden, of course, on retirement from the game, would go on to compile his Wisden's Almanac which has become the cricketer's bible in respect of facts, figures, statistics and analysis of all things cricket.

Having made investigations into the composition of the Glasgow team, it appears to have been a Clydesdale XI beefed up with a selection of seasoned English professional cricketers and invited stars of the day to make up a twenty-two to take on an All England select.

Clydesdale's team had players of note whose representative statistics reflect their capabilities.

J Morrison played for Scotland (1852-1858), **Archibald McCraw** for Scotland (1852), **Archibald Campbell** for Scotland (1852-1854), **E Morrison** for Scotland (1852-1858) and **William Connochie** for Scotland (1852-1858), Colonel Buchanan's Scotland Team (1860), Caledonian Club (1861) and the Gentlemen of Scotland (1862).

One of the invited players was a **Thomas Moncrieffe** who was something of a cricketing superstar of the time. He was Sir Thomas Moncrieffe, 7th Baronet of Moncrieffe, and he had the distinction of playing for the Marylebone Cricket Club (1841-1855), Gentlemen of the North (1852), Officers of the Guard (1841), L to Z (1844), W Mills' XI (1844), R Grimston's XI (1846), Scotland (1849-1855), Lord Guernsey's XI (1850), I Zingari (1850-1862), Gentlemen of England (1852), Kelso (1852) and the Earl of Stamford's Team (1854-1855).

His four grandsons, Gerald Ward, John Ward, Robert Ward and Reginald Ward, and his son-in-law, William Ward, the Earl of Dudley, also went on to play First Class cricket. Robert Ward went on to become the son-in-law of Lord Acheson whose relations were the various Foljambes, all of whom also went on to play First Class cricket.

The seasoned English professionals were men such as **Andrew Crossland** who turned out for Yorkshire (1844-1855), North of England (1853), All England Eleven (1853-1857), Dalton (1844-1852), Bradford (1848), Ripon (1848), Leeds (1848-1850), Huddersfield and Dalton (1850-1851), Players of Yorkshire (1850), Staffordshire (1851), Scotland (1851-1858), Birmingham (1851-1853), Liverpool Olympus (1852), Broughton (1852-1854), Sleaford (1852-1853), Northumberland Club (1852), St Helens (1853), Liverpool (1853-1855), Rotherham (1853-1854), Gentlemen of Yorkshire (1854), Rochdale (1854), Langton Wold (1855), Hull (1855-1866), Whitehaven (1856), Melton Mowbray (1856), York (1856-1863), Bristol (1856), Stoke-on-Trent (1856), Wakefield (1857), Boston (England) (1857), Eastwell (1858), Gainsborough (1860), Hull Mechanics Institution (1867) and Hornsea (1871).

George Armitage played for Yorkshire (1850-1853), Single (1849), North of England (1849-1850), Dalton (1844-1852), Huddersfield (1848-1850), Bradford (1848-1851), Leeds (1848), Rugby (1849), Atherstone (1849), Leamington (1849-1850), Manchester (1850), Huddersfield and Dalton (1850-1851), Gentlemen of Warwickshire (1850), Langton Wold (1850), Birmingham (1850-1855), Broughton (1851-1853), Sleaford (1851-1853), Staffordshire (1851), Newburgh Park (1851), Scotland (1851-1852), Liverpool (1853), Cirencester (1853), Spalding (1853-1855), St Helens (1854), Dudley (1854-1855) and Lincolnshire (1854).

William Usherwood was originally from Halifax and played for Scotland (1849-1858), Northumberland Club (1851), Grange (1856-1859), Clydesdale (1859) and Colonel Buchanan's Scotland Team (1860).

Edmund Sopp was a wicketkeeper from Haywards Heath who played for Sussex (1843-1847), Petworth (1844-1845), Players (1845), Players of Sussex (1843), West Sussex (1844), Birmingham (1847-1849), All England Eleven (1848), Carlisle (1850), Scotland (1850-1852), Northumberland Club (1851), Sussex (1851), Kelso (1852), Richmond (Yorkshire) (1854), Monmouthshire (1855)and the United Ireland Eleven (1858).

It is of historical importance to draw attention to these cricketers, as well as acknowledging a great many others, for their presence and participation for all these clubs and selects in these early matches are the relevant building blocks that ensured the creation and establishment of cricket as a national team sport, not only in Scotland, but in England and Ireland as well.

In the game itself, which was drawn, **Jonny Wisden** took 21 wickets, which is a fairly impressive feat, but Wisden's playing career was even more so. He played for the following: Sussex (1845-1863), Kent (1854), Middlesex (1859-1863), Players (1845-1859), England (1846-1859), All England Eleven (1848-1851), Fast Bowlers (1849), Single (1849-1858), North of England (1849-1850), Under 36 (1850), South of England (1851-1863), Manchester (1852-1857), Surrey and Sussex (1852-1857), United England Eleven (1853-1862) and Kent and Sussex (1856-1859).

Wisden, along with **George Parr** and **William Caffyn**, were members of the first ever overseas cricket tour when an expeditionary England side travelled to the Americas and played in Canada and the United States in 1859. George Parr was a stalwart of the All England XI and was the captain of the team for this tour. He captained England's second tour to Australia and New Zealand in 1864, returning home unbeaten. William Caffyn was instrumental in the early development of Australian cricket and became the coach of the Melbourne Cricket Club from 1864 to 1874.

The first English overseas touring side on board ship at Liverpool:
Standing: Robert Carpenter, William Caffyn, Tom Lockyer;
Middle row: John Wisden, HH Stephenson, George Parr, James Grundy, Julius Caesar, Thomas Hayward, John Jackson;
Front row: Alfred Diver, John Lillywhite.

By 1860, Clydesdale had become one of the premier cricket teams in Scotland and THE premier cricket team in the west of the country. Later in the same decade, the cricketers had begun to play association football during the winter months. It was originally seen as a way to keep fit during the off-season, use the ground and also keep the club, and its members, together all the year round.

Before long, Clydesdale had established themselves with a reputation as a leading club within association football. Queen's Park Football Club, the original pioneers of association football in Scotland, and freshly enthused about the sport after their sortie as a Scotland team against England in the first football international in November 1872, were finding it increasingly difficult to find opposition to play against domestically and asked a number of football playing cricket clubs to attend a meeting within the Dewars Hotel in Bridge Street, Glasgow on 13th March 1873 with a view to founding an association of like-minded clubs who would introduce a governance structure for the sport and its member clubs.

The clubs in attendance were Queen's Park, Clydesdale, Vale of Leven,

Dumbreck, Third Lanark, Eastern and Granville with Kilmarnock sending a letter of interest to join. This meeting saw the foundation of the Scottish Football Association, and during this meeting, Archibald Campbell, the founder of Clydesdale Cricket Club, was elected the first president, and two other Clydesdale members, Ebenezer Hendry and William Gibb, were elected onto the first committee.

In October of the same year, 16 clubs including 13 cricket clubs, embarked on the quest for the first Scottish Cup. The original clubs were Alexandra Athletic, Blythswood, Callander, Clydesdale, Dumbarton, Dumbreck, Eastern, Granville, Kilmarnock, Queen's Park, Renton, Rovers, Southern, 3rd Lanark Rifle Volunteers, Vale of Leven and Western.

Clydesdale had Scottish international players Frederick Anderson, John McPherson, James J Lang, James Tassie Richmond in the forward line, David Wotherspoon in defence and Robert W Gardner as captain and goalkeeper, and were viewed as favourites for the cup, along with Queen's Park.

Clydesdale, were at the time, the only club strong enough to be expected to give Queen's Park a good game. Clydesdale beat Granville 6-0 in the first round and having faced Third Lanark in the quarter-final and two replays, eventually beat them 2-0. Clydesdale then played Blythswood in a home semi-final in December 1873 and won 4-0 to face Queen's Park in the first Scottish Cup Final.

Clydesdale's goalkeeper and Captain, Robert W Gardner, had enjoyed seven unbroken years of clean sheets as the Queen's Park goalkeeper, however, in the final at Hampden on 21st March 1874, he lost his record against his old club, the score being 2-0. By way of consolation, 1874 saw Clydesdale break Queen's Park's perfect clean sheet record and also saw them thump Notts County 6-0.

Also in 1874, the land-owner, Sir John Stirling Maxwell, told Clydesdale it would have to move from its Kinning Park location due to the necessary expansion of the Caledonian Railway with marshalling yards, sidings and coal depots. A choice of locations was offered for a new ground - Paisley Road around Ibrox, the new Queen's Park at Langside, or the fields to the south of Pollokshields called Titwood. The club chose Titwood.

The final cricket match at Kinning Park was played in September 1875 while Clydesdale's footballers played at Kinning Park for one more winter with the final game being against the ground's successors, Rangers, on Saturday 18th March 1876.

In the 1874/75 Scottish Cup, Clydesdale lost to Queen's Park 1-0 in a second semi-final replay and in the 1875/76 Scottish Cup campaign, Clydesdale again met their nemesis, Queen's Park, in the third round and lost 2-0. Clydesdale's football fortunes faded and the section was discontinued in 1890 after being thrashed 6-1 by Northern in the first round of the Scottish Cup.

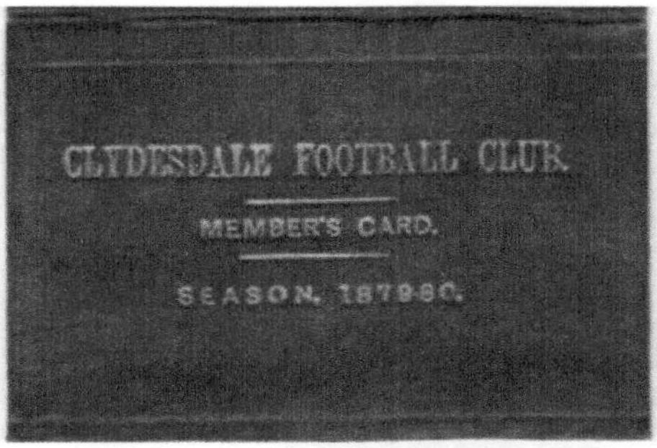

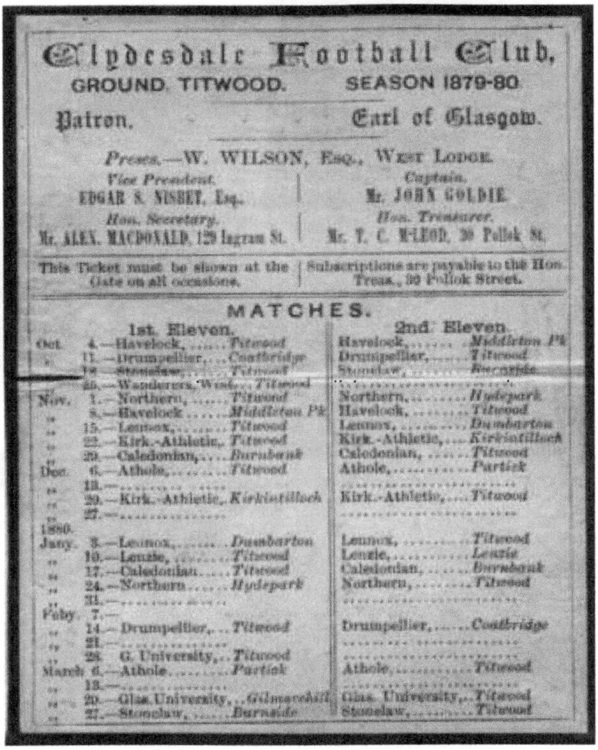

Clydesdale Football Club,

GROUND TITWOOD. SEASON 1879-80

Patron. Earl of Glasgow.

Pres.,—W. WILSON, Esq., West Lodge.

Vice President. EDGAR S. NISBET, Esq. | Captain. Mr. JOHN GOLDIE.

Hon. Secretary. Mr. ALEX. MACDONALD, 129 Ingram St. | Hon. Treasurer. Mr. T. C. M'LEOD, 30 Pollok St.

This Ticket must be shown at the Gate on all occasions. | Subscriptions are payable to the Hon. Treas., 30 Pollok Street.

MATCHES.

		1st. Eleven.		2nd. Eleven.	
Oct.	4.—	Havelock,	Titwood	Havelock,	Middleton Pk
"	11.—	Drumpellier,	Coatbridge	Drumpellier,	Titwood
"	18.—	Stonelaw,	Titwood	Stonelaw,	Burnside
"	25.—	Wanderers, [illegible]	Titwood		
Nov.	1.—	Northern,	Titwood	Northern,	Hydepark
"	8.—	Havelock	Middleton Pk	Havelock,	Titwood
"	15.—	Lennox,	Titwood	Lennox,	Dumbarton
"	22.—	Kirk.-Athletic,	Titwood	Kirk.-Athletic,	Kirkintilloch
"	29.—	Caledonian,	Burnbank	Caledonian,	Titwood
Dec.	6.—	Athole,	Titwood	Athole,	Partick
"	13.—				
"	20.—	Kirk.-Athletic,	Kirkintilloch	Kirk.-Athletic,	Titwood
"	27.—				
1880. Jany.	3.—	Lennox,	Dumbarton	Lennox,	Titwood
"	10.—	Lenzie,	Titwood	Lenzie,	Lenzie
"	17.—	Caledonian	Titwood	Caledonian,	Burnbank
"	24.—	Northern	Hydepark	Northern,	Titwood
"	31.—				
Feby.	7.—				
"	14.—	Drumpellier,	Titwood	Drumpellier,	Coatbridge
"	21.—				
"	28.	G. University,	Titwood		
March	6.—	Athole	Partick	Athole,	Titwood
"	13.—				
"	20.—	Glas. University,	Gilmorehill	Glas. University,	Titwood
"	27.—	Stonelaw,	Burnside	Stonelaw,	Titwood

CLYDESDALE

Having spent a considerable amount of time researching the comings and goings of the various crickets clubs and how their respective members turned to football during the winter months, whether it was by the playing of the association or rugby versions, I did notice that the clubs were playing fixtures in all three sports mainly by arrangement.

Apart from the fledgling association football Scottish Cup competition and the English Football Association Challenge Cup and their initial cup draw fixtures, clubs played friendlies. The structured league and cup competition formats that we take for granted in the 21st Century were non-existent. The creation of league competition for cricket, football and rugby did not appear until the early 1890s.

When you consider that 21st Century fixture secretaries have the benefit of telephone, text and e-mail to organise matches, and that most governing bodies provide the majority of competitive fixtures for any given season well in advance, one cannot help but admire the diligence of the 19th Century club fixture secretaries and how they arranged so many matches for their members to participate in.

This admiration of the efforts of these 19th Century fixture secretaries also leads to an appreciation of an aspect I hadn't really considered before. The simplistic structure of their fixture calendars has remained a principle of cricket in the west of Scotland for over 150 years. The simple nature of having a mirror-image fixture calendar whereby Team A plays Team B at Ground A and Team B 2nd XI plays Team A 2nd XI at Ground B on the same day, and then reversing these fixtures for the second half of the season, has remained as a lasting legacy.

With Clydesdale's move to Titwood in 1876, there have been many sporting highlights and historical events on the ground. Some are well known, and others that have just been lost in the mists of time.

In 1880, a few days after playing the inaugural Test match against England at the Kennington Oval, the original touring Australian side travelled to Titwood to play a two day game. It is the Australians first sojourn into Scotland and the match was held on the 10th and 11th September.

Depending on the sources, it is a Clydesdale Invitational XVIII with players from West of Scotland and Drumpellier, or a Glasgow XVIII. Whatever the name, the home side batted first in front of 7,000 spectators and posted 224. The Australians replied with 111, and having been asked to follow-on, scored 47 for 1 when play came to a halt. In some cricket data-bases, the match is classified as a draw, but going by practices of the time, the first

SEASON 1875-6.

CLYDESDALE FOOTBALL CLUB.

Patron—EARL OF GLASGOW.

President—J. C. WAKEFIELD, Esq., of Eastwood.

Vice-President—G. DONALD, Esq.

Committee—Messrs R. GARDNER, A. MACBRUTHAR, and D. SINCLAIR.

Honorary-Treasurer—Mr. D. WOTHERSPOON, 19 South Portland Street.

Honorary-Secretary—Mr. D. SINCLAIR, 62 Waterloo Street (East).

LIST OF MATCHES.

FIRST ELEVEN.			SECOND ELEVEN.		
Date.	Club.	Ground.	Date.	Club.	Ground.
Oct. 2,	Opening Match,	Kinning Park.	Oct. 2,	Opening Match,	Kinning Park.
" 9,			" 9,		
" 16,	Rangers, - -	Kinning Park.	" 16,	2nd Rangers, -	Burnbank.
" 23,			" 23,		
" 30,	Vale of Leven, -	Alexandria.	" 30,	2nd Vale of Leven,	Kinning Park.
Nov. 6,	3rd L.R.V., - -	Cathkin Park.	Nov. 6,	2nd 3rd L.R.V., -	Kinning Park.
" 13,			" 13,		
" 20,	Alexandra Athletic,	Kinning Park.	" 20,	2nd Alexandra Athletic,	Alexandra Park.
" 27,	Dumbreck, - -	Thornhill.	" 27,	2nd Dumbreck, -	Kinning Park.
Dec. 4,	Queen's Park, -	Kinning Park.	Dec. 4,	2nd Queen's Park,	Hampden Park.
" 11,			" 11,		
" 18,	Western, - -	Kinning Park.	" 18,	2nd Western, -	Regent Park.
" 25,	Queen's Park		" 25,		
Jan. 1,			Jan. 1,		
" 8,			" 8,		
" 15,	Rangers, - -	Burnbank.	" 15,	2nd Rangers, -	Kinning Park.
" 22,	3rd L.R.V., -	Kinning Park.	" 22,	2nd 3rd L.R.V., -	Cathkin Park.
" 29,	Dumbreck, -	Kinning Park.	" 29,	2nd Dumbreck, -	Thornhill.
Feb. 5,	Queen's Park, -	Hampden Park.	Feb. 5,	2nd Queen's Park.	Kinning Park.
" 12,			" 12,		
" 19,			" 19,		
" 26,	Vale of Leven, -	Kinning Park.	" 26,	2nd Vale of Leven,	Alexandria.
Mar. 4,	Western, -	Kinning Park.	Mar. 4,	2nd Western, -	Regent Park.
" 11,			" 11,		
" 18,			" 18,		
" 25,	Closing Match, -	Kinning Park.	" 25,	Closing Match, -	Kinning Park.

This Ticket (which is not Transferable) must be shown at the Gate on all Match Days.

Subscriptions to be paid to the Treasurer on or before 1st November.

innings score in an uncompleted two-innings match resulted in a famous victory for Clydesdale (Glasgow).

But nine years later in 1889, Clydesdale's cricket had temporarily declined with tennis threatening to replace it. The cricket revived and local tennis clubs still compete for the 'Clydesdale Trophy'.

After the association football section's demise in 1890, rugby football appeared at Titwood. In 1896/97, Clydesdale Rugby Club shared the Scottish league championship with Jedforest and Watsonians. Five Clydesdale players went on to win Scottish rugby football caps: T L Hendry (1893, 95), E Spencer (1898), J M Dykes (1898-1902), J A Bell (1901-02) and J Robertson (1908).

Blythswood

Blythswood was another "Big House" cricket club that also played football. The cricket club was formed in 1854 and was initially based in the grounds of Blythswood House on the Ranfield Estate. Blythswood House was situated on the right bank of the river Cart, near its junction with the Clyde. The house itself was built in 1821 by Archibald Campbell of Blythswood, the MP for the Glasgow District of Burghs, which at the time comprehended Glasgow, Rutherglen, Renfrew and Dumbarton.

Blythswood House was also at the forefront of modern science. From 1892 to 1905 it housed an experimental laboratory that was used to research the development of X-rays and cathode rays and early inroads into the fields of spectroscopy and radioactivity.

The house was demolished in 1935 and the surrounding lands were turned into what is now the Renfrew Golf Club. The Blythswood House land interests, outwith the Ranfield Estate, comprised of around 500 acres in what is now Glasgow city centre and stretched westwards from what is West Nile Street, along Argyle Street to Dumbarton Road. Renfield Street is named so as a variant of the Ranfield Estate name and Blythswood Square is also named after the house. Glasgow Central Station, along with a number of other railway stations, all now stand on what was once Blythswood House land.

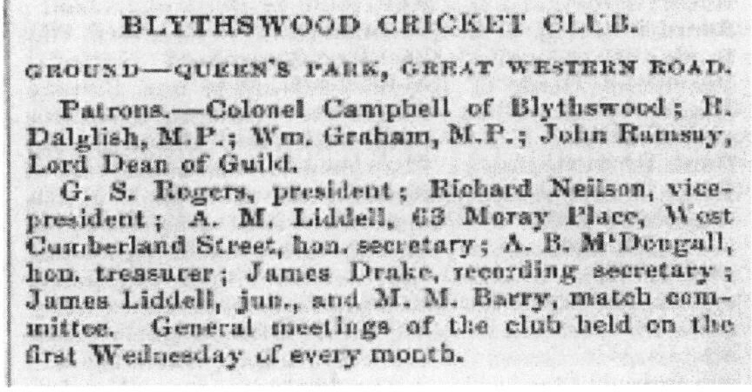

BLYTHSWOOD CRICKET CLUB.

GROUND—QUEEN'S PARK, GREAT WESTERN ROAD.

Patrons.—Colonel Campbell of Blythswood; R. Dalglish, M.P.; Wm. Graham, M.P.; John Ramsay, Lord Dean of Guild.

G. S. Rogers, president; Richard Neilson, vice-president; A. M. Liddell, 63 Moray Place, West Cumberland Street, hon. secretary; A. B. M'Dougall, hon. treasurer; James Drake, recording secretary; James Liddell, jun., and M. M. Barry, match committee. General meetings of the club held on the first Wednesday of every month.

The cricket club was the patronage of Colonel Colin Campbell and with more clubs appearing in the western extremity of the city in the 1860s, he took the decision to have the playing of the club's cricket to be at the Queen's Park ground just off Great Western Road.

There was a brief spell at Springgrove before moving to the 18 acre expanse of Burnbank, the home of many other clubs at the time, which, incidentally, was owned by the Blythswood Estate and drew feus from the various clubs that leased "pitches" on it.

BLYTHSWOOD CRICKET CLUB.

(LATE SPRINGGROVE).

GROUND—BURNBANK, GREAT WESTERN ROAD.

Patrons—R. Dalglish, Esq., M.P.; Sir Michael Shaw Stewart, Bart.; Lieut.-Col. Holmes, Provost Shaw, Maryhill, Councillor James Morrison. Hon. secretary, R. H. Sinclair, 64 Grove Street; hon. treasurer, Jas. Murray; committee of management, J. Mitchell, J. S. P. Bain, G. C. Martin, J. Jamieson, W. C. Davidson. Annual subscription, 15s.

As time passed, Burnbank itself was swallowed up by the demand for housing to meet the expansion of the city. The cricket club moved again westwards to be based at Westburn Park in Kelvinside before returning home to the Blythswood Estate in the 1890s.

BLYTHSWOOD CRICKET CLUB.—*President*—William Brown; *Vice-President*—P. G. Bell; *Captain*—W. B. Smith; *Vice-Captain*—George Tripney; *Secretary*—J. A. Robertson; *Treasurer*—William Richardson, 21 Fulbar street; *Match Committee*—Committee of Office-bearers. Ground—Blythswood Park.

The football club started in 1873 and was a founder member of the Scottish Football Association as well as being one of the original sixteen teams that participated in the first Scottish Cup competition. The football team also played at Westburn Park in Kelvinside but folded in 1879. The football team got to the semi-final stage of the inaugural Scottish Cup where they met Clydesdale.

I discovered a press cutting of a match report for this cup semi-final of 13th December 1873 and have reproduced it.

CLYDESDALE v. BLYTHSWOOD - Played on Kinning Park, the ground of the Clydesdale, and resulted as an easy victory for the elder club by four goals to nil. The ground was very soft and did not show of the Association game to advantage. At a few minutes before three o'clock both teams faced each other for the first time, and a single glance showed to which side the weight leaned - the senior club being a couple of stone heavier all over. The Blythswood were successful in winning the toss, and this necessitated their opponents to play against a strong, gusty wind, which blew across the ground the whole time the game lasted. At the outset it looked as if the strangers were going to have the best of the game, as, with the wind in their favour, they kept the ball well in neutral ground for some time. The back-play of the Clydesdale, however, was equal to the occasion. In about half an hour after the game began, in spite of the wind and the steady forward play of one or two of the Blythswood forwards, including Messrs. W. Phillips and Brues, a splendid rush by the whole of the Clydesdale forwards was too much for the younger club, and Mr. Gibb, by a fine, steady shot, scored the first goal for the Clydesdale. On ends being changed the latter club made another fine charge, and so well was the ball "middled" by the half-backs and backs that another goal was soon kicked by Mr. A. Taylor. Shortly after this the third goal was kicked at the upper end by Mr. J. Wilson, but the ball struck the hand of the Blythswood goal-keeper before it went under the tape. Shortly before time was called, another goal was successfully kicked by Mr. A. Taylor, the ball being finely centred by Messrs. Gibb, Gardener, Wilson, and Hendry. After this goal the umpires agreed to cease hostilities, as the light was very bad, leaving the Clydesdale victorious by four goals by none. The following were the teams: - BLYTHSWOOD. - J. McDougal (goal, captain), G. Phillips, W. Davidson, backs; W. Bain and Brues, half-backs; J. Wright, J. Phillips, W. Gibb, D. McPhun, A. Smith, and J. Stevenson, forwards. CLYDESDALE - G. Webster (goal), J. Gardener (capt.), A. Raeburn, backs; D. Wotherspoon, J. Stanley, half-backs; J. Wilson, W. Gibb, F. Anderson, A. Laing, A.Taylor, E. Hendry, forwards. The Clydesdale will now meet the Queen's Park for the final tie for the Cup.

BLYTHSWOOD

Alexandra

Alexandra Cricket Club Ground, Queen's park, Langside road.

Alexandra originally started as a cricket club in 1866 and their ground was in Langside Road, Queens Park. The club was eventually forced to move as their ground was required for urban development and ended up at Kennyhill Park in what is now called Alexandra Park on the north-eastern side of Glasgow.

GLASGOW ALEXANDRA ATHLETIC CLUB.
Instituted 1873.

GROUNDS—KENNYHILL, CUMBERNAULD ROAD.

Patrons—The Right Hon. the Earl of Glasgow, Colonel Buchanan of Drumpellier, Colonel Moore, Garrowbank; Major Clark, Dennistoun; Robert Dalglish, Esq.; John Clark, Esq., Dennistoun; Alex. M'Casland, Esq., Gartcraig; Robert Boustead, Esq., Dunoon; William R. Hill, Esq., Barlanark; W. J. Donald, Esq., Annan. Honorary president, James M'Casland, Esq., Gartcraig; president, Thomas Cross; vice president, Robert Edington; captain, William M'Elroy; vice-captain, John Graham; secretary, William Dick, 73 Whitevale Street; treasurer, Wm. M'Arthur; directors, Eben. M'Elroy, David Graham, John R. Hastie, P. Kinnear, and Robert Hardie; match committee, William Coubrough, John Graham, Alex. M'Vicar, L. Baird, and William Dick, secretary; auditors, Andrew Allan and William Roy. Annual subscription, £1 1s.; honorary members, £1 1s.

The football team began in 1873, had limited success and then folded in 1884.

Alexandra's football strip was yet another example of innovation and it is a handsome outfit.

ALEXANDRA ATHLETIC

Alexandria

This short-lived football team was actually registered with the Scottish Football Association as Alexandria Cricket Club. The football team played their home games at Balloch Road from 1877-1879.

Dumbreck

Dumbreck Cricket Club played in the grounds of Ibroxhill House in what is now Bellahouston Park. All the lands of Dumbreck had originally belonged to Robert Smith, founder of the Thistle Bank. He had inherited Dumbreck from his uncle William Wardrop, a Glasgow merchant who had acquired the estate in 1790.

The cricket club was formed in 1868 and like elsewhere, the cricketers formed a football team in 1872. They played in the first Scottish Cup and were one of the eight founder members of the Scottish Football Association.

The entire club folded in 1879

The 176 acres were sold by the Trustees of the estate to Glasgow Corporation for the sum of £50,000.00 to form what was then the city's largest public park.

Glasgow Corporation anticipated the needs of its rapidly spreading city and extended the park further in 1901 by purchasing additional land from Sir John Stirling Maxwell of the Pollok Estate for £2,824.00. In 1903, the adjoining lands of Ibroxhill were purchased by the Corporation for £40,220.00.

DUMBRECK

Dumbarton

Dumbarton Cricket Club was formed in 1868, and in 1872, a group of young cricketers resolved to form a football club after watching a match between Queen's Park and neighbouring Vale of Leven.

A year later Dumbarton Football Club registered with the Scottish Football Association and in 1879, they moved to Boghead Park. For five years they remained unbeaten at home, establishing themselves as one of the leading clubs in the West of Scotland.

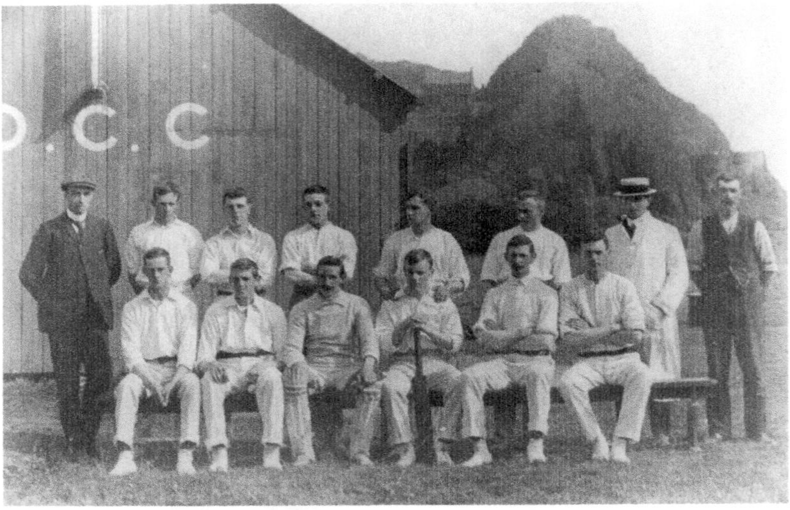

They appeared in six Scottish Football Association Cup finals, winning the tournament in 1883. They then went on to thrash English Football Association Cup holders Blackburn Rovers 6-1 to be hailed as unofficial champions of Great Britain.

DUMBARTON

Renton

Originally drawn to football when the cricket season finished, Renton was the cricketing oasis between Dumbarton and Alexandria and formed in 1872. The local area was a nursery of Scottish football, with Renton's neighbours, Vale of Leven and Dumbarton, producing the outstanding teams of the age.

In 1888 Renton beat Cambuslang 6-1 in the Scottish Cup final to record their second cup win. In the 1888 English Football Association Cup final, underdogs West Bromwich Albion beat Preston North End. West Bromwich Albion, obviously feeling exceedingly brave, issued a challenge to Renton. They would come to Scotland and meet Renton on a neutral ground to determine which club was indeed the better and deserved to be the "Champions of the United Kingdom" – and the World.

Renton accepted the offer, and on Saturday 19th May 1888, the sides met at Cathkin Park. The match was played in appalling conditions with Renton running out 4-1 winners in front of a record 10,000 fans. Renton's team on the day included a 19 year old lad called Neil McCallum, who later that year would score the first ever goal for Celtic.

A sign proclaiming Renton 'Champions of the World' appeared above their pavilion at Tontine Park. Two weeks later, Renton cemented their claims of world domination by beating Preston North End in an exhibition game. It was this Preston North End team, who, the following season, won the first 'Double' in England, and with it the nickname "The Invincibles".

RENTON

RENTON FOOTBALL TEAM
"Champions of the World"
R. Kelso, half back   A. Hannah, back   J. Lindsay, Goal   A. McCall (Captain), back   D. McKechnie, half back
N. McCallum and H. Campbell, right wing   J. Kelly, centre half back   J. Campbell, centre   J. McCall and J. McNee, left wing
Winners of the Scottish and Glasgow Charity Cups

Kilmarnock

The cricket club is one of the oldest in Scotland and can trace its origins back to 1852, when four enthusiasts of the sport came together to promote the formation of a local team. They founded the Kilmarnock Winton Cricket Club, though the Winton part of the name was eventually dropped.

The club began life at Holmquarry Road with their own pitch and clubhouse. They remained there until 1904, when the land was needed for the town's new power station and tramway depot. At that point the club moved to a new pitch at Kirkstyle which remained the club's home until the move to Bellsland in 2000. In 2012, Kilmarnock moved to a designated purpose-built facility at Scott Ellis Field.

CRICKET CLUBS.

KILMARNOCK CRICKET CLUB.

President—William Thomson. | Captain—James Dickie.

Secretary and Treasurer—Thos. Ferguson.

The football club aspect dates back to 1869, which makes Kilmarnock the second oldest surviving football club in Scotland after Queen's Park. The football club was originally founded by young cricketers to provide a winter activity, and they initially played according to the rugby code but switched to association football. When the various Kilmarnock cricket and football teams separated their interests in 1899, with the football team moving into its own ground, its starting origins are reflected by calling it Rugby Park.

In 1984, I was an 18 year old who had broken into Clydesdale's 1st team and I was enjoying the opportunity in its long hot summer.

Clydesdale were due to play Kilmarnock at Kirkstyle on Saturday 11th August and I was awoken by a news report on the radio that Kilmarnock's clubhouse had been burnt to the ground overnight. I went round to Clydesdale where it was confirmed that Kilmarnock's clubhouse had indeed been burnt to the ground, the 1st XI game was cancelled but the 2nd XI game would be going ahead at Clydesdale that afternoon.

My memories of that day are of seeing an almost entire membership of Kilmarnock Cricket Club at Clydesdale to mourn the loss of their clubhouse, console themselves and obviously make arrangements and hold discussions on what had to be done to repair/replace the damage.

The images that are still crystal clear, nearly 30 years on, are of the grief etched into the faces of the Kilmarnock members. It wasn't the clubhouse being burnt down that was the problem as it could be rebuilt, but it was the loss of the records, memorabilia, photographs and archives that couldn't be replaced and how 132 years worth of history had been lost as a result of wanton vandalism.

It made me appreciate that we should protect and preserve what we simply take for granted – our collective history, and once it is lost, we can never replace it.

KILMARNOCK

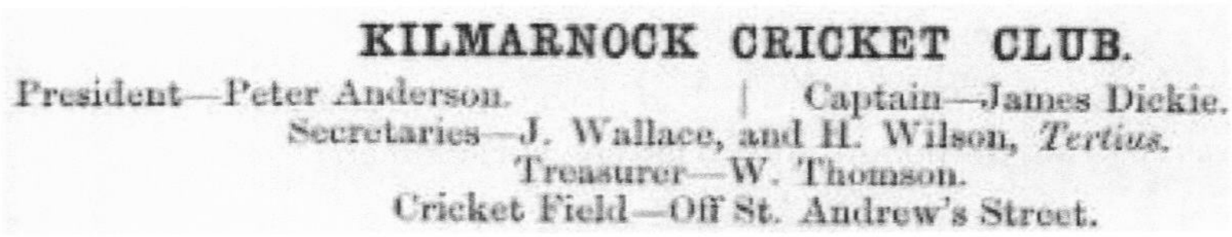

KILMARNOCK CRICKET CLUB.

President—Peter Anderson. | Captain—James Dickie.
Secretaries—J. Wallace, and H. Wilson, *Tertius.*
Treasurer—W. Thomson.
Cricket Field—Off St. Andrew's Street.

Kilmarnock 1879

Vale of Leven

In the early days of Scottish football, Vale of Leven, another cricket club, based in Alexandria, and their near neighbours, Renton, were the real powers in the land. Vale was formed as a cricket club in 1852 and to continue the club during the winter months, the cricketers turned to playing association football in 1872.

Vale went on to win the Scottish Football Association Cup three times in succession in 1877, 1878 and 1879 and went on to become founder members when the Scottish Football League was formed in 1890.

The club still exists at Millburn Park, with the cricketers playing in the Western District Cricket Union Championship and the footballers, in their own facility beside the cricket pitch, playing in the Scottish Junior Football Association West Central Division Two.

Another sporting interest of note was that the club also played shinty in its early days and won the Celtic Society Cup in 1879.

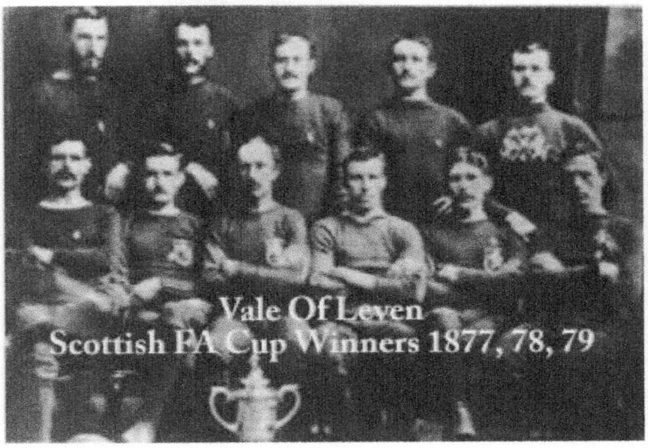

VALE OF LEVEN

Whiteinch

Whiteinch was a shipbuilding district west of Glasgow city centre. In 1867, a cricket team appeared in the area called Glasgow Derby. The club started off at Belmont Park, at the beginning of Great Western Road, and as a result of constant residential building projects, moved westwards to Regent's Park, just off Dumbarton Road.

DERBY CRICKET CLUB, GLASGOW.
Instituted 1867.
GROUND—BELMONT PARK, GREAT WESTERN ROAD.

Patron—John Hoggan, Esq.; president, George B. Sawers; vice-president, John T. Sharkey; secretary, W. M. Marr, 17 Stanley Street; treasurer, J. W. Holm. Committee—W. Dewar, D. A. Crawford, Jas. M'Nab, and W. M. Marr. Annual subscription, 10s. for ordinary members; and 7s. 6d. for hon. members.

The club were moved and moved again due to continual construction work and found themselves a final home in Westburn Park. As was becoming increasingly common practice at other clubs, the cricketers turned to football for the winter months and formed a team in 1874 and called themselves Whiteinch to signify where they were based.

DERBY CRICKET CLUB.
GROUND—REGENT'S PARK, OFF DUMBARTON ROAD.
Instituted 1867.

Patrons—The most noble the Marquis of Lorne, M.P., and Alexander Whitelaw, Esq., M.P.; president, Charles Norman Crichton; vice-president, Jas. J. Freeborn; secretary, Neil M'Neill, 103 St. Vincent Street; treasurer, James Paterson; committee, Neil M'Neill, James J. Freeborn, James Paterson, Arthur C. Green, Charles Norman Crichton, William Law, H. E. Clifford, and George Findlay. Annual subscription one guinea.

WHITEINCH

The football team had limited success and folded in 1879. The cricket club appeared to fold around 1890.

In this modern age of logo branding and corporate identity, Whiteinch were pioneers in the field. The club had a one-inch wide white stripe sewn into the left sleeve of their shirt to signify the team and where they came from - Whiteinch. Brilliant!

Pollokshields

Pollokshields Cricket Club was another example where cricketers were also playing association football during the winter months.

The cricket club seems to appear about 1871. The football team was formed in 1875, however, the whole club disappears in 1890. The club was operating in Pollokshields long before Clydesdale's move to the area, but due to the geography, Pollokshields Cricket Club's original ground, Prince's Park, lay less than 900 yards south-east of where Clydesdale's ground was at Kinning Park.

CLYDESDALE CRICKET CLUB.

Instituted 1848.

GROUND—KINNING PARK, PAISLEY ROAD.

Earl of Glasgow, patron; J. C. Wakefield, Esq., president; G. Donald, Esq., vice-president; general committee, A. Campbell, J. Brownlie, D. Swan, G. Webster, and E. Hendry; hon. treasurer, J. M'Arly, Pollok Street; hon. secretary, E. Hendry, 123 Argyle Street.

POLLOKSHIELDS CRICKET CLUB.

GROUND—PRINCE'S PARK, POLLOKSHIELDS.

Patron—Right Hon. H. A. Bruce, M.P.; president, Peter Dunn; vice-president, Thos. Gardner; treasurer, Robert Howie; committee, P. Dunn, T. Gardner, J. Laughland, A. M'Culloch, M. M. Graham; secy., Mungo M. Graham, Rowanlea, Pollokshields.

Prince's Park appears to have been located at the end of Prince's Street in Pollokshields. Prince's Street no longer exists as it has been extended into what is now called McCulloch Street. As far as I can deduce, Prince's Park was very close to where the Pollokshields Bowling Club is now currently situated at the bottom of St. Johns Road.

The club moved from Prince's Park, and I can only surmise as a result of the ground being required for the building of the many residential properties that sprung up in the area from the late 1870s onwards, and played for three years at Lorne Park 1877-1880 before finally moving into the Pollok Estate in 1880 until folding in 1890.

It seems that many of the cricket clubs whose members formed sections to play football during the winter months ceased to do so in 1890, which coincidentally was the same year of the creation of the professional Scottish Football League.

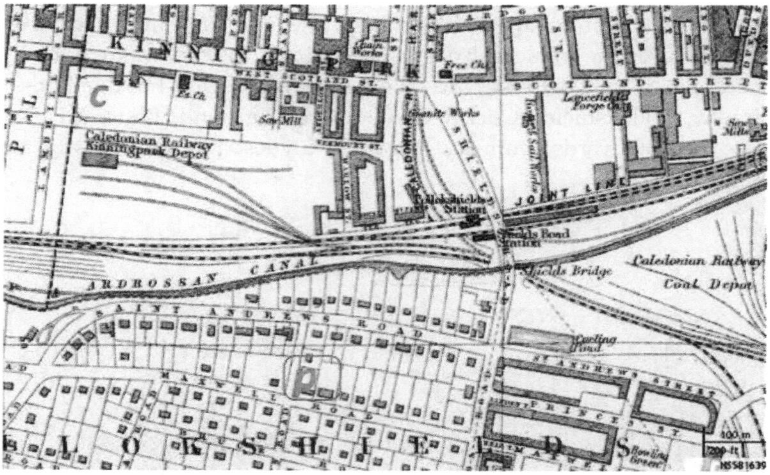

POLLOKSHIELDS

The football team played in a strip that is definitely a century ahead of its time. It certainly was eye-catching, to say the least, and also very distinctive.

Airdrie

Airdrie Cricket Club was founded in 1860.

As the new sport of football was becoming popular with cricketers to play during the winter months, a football section was formed in 1868 and initially played as Excelsior. The football separated from the cricket in 1878 and played as Airdrionians FC until adopting the title of Airdrieonians in 1881.

After the separation in 1878, Airdrie Cricket Club continued playing football until folding in 1890, the year of creation of the Scottish Football League. The cricketers had very distinctive strips and played in blue & scarlet from 1868-1880, then red & blue striped shirts and white shorts from 1880-1882, in an all-white number from 1882-1884 and finally, in a very daring white shirt with green tassels and white shorts from 1884-1890.

The footballers played in blue and white striped shirts and socks with white shorts.

The cricketers played at a number of grounds such as Academy Park 1868-1878, Cairnhill Park 1878-1881, Rochsolloch 1881 - 1884, and finally at Smiths Fields from 1884-1890.

AIRDRIE

AIRDRIE

Dunfermline Cricket Club

Dunfermline Cricket Club was founded in 1857. The club has mainly played at its ground, Lady's Mill Park, however, the original football section has played elsewhere. Lady's Mill Park was renamed McKane Park after a wealthy benefactor and patron of the club, John McKane.

The football section was founded in 1874 with the intent of being a way to keep the cricketers fit during the winter months.

In 1885, a demand that only members of the cricket club could play football, resulted in the footballers leaving en masse and forming Dunfermline Athletic Football Club. However, in 1891, the cricket club disbanded the operation of a Senior XI and turned to playing Junior football instead.

The cricket club approached a local football club, South-side Athletic, who were groundless, and offered them the use of Lady's Mill, on the condition that they changed their name to Dunfermline and operated as a Junior club. This Junior club folded in 1901. The cricketers cum footballers of Dunfermline played at Towngreen from 1874-1879 and at Lady's Mill Park from 1879 to 1901. The football club also used Broomhead and Brucefield Parks on an infrequent basis.

As a result of being created, free from the oppressive restrictions of its parent cricket club, Dunfermline Athletic Football Club started off at East End Park in 1885. However, between 1892 and 1896, and during the 1898-99 season, the club didn't run a Senior XI as a result of low crowds and minimal income. To compensate matters, the club operated mainly as a Junior side from 1892-1900.

DUNFERMLINE

During the First World War, the Junior XI was restarted in 1915 and continued until 1918 and the cessation of hostilities. During this period, Dunfermline Athletic Football Club played at West End and Blackburn Parks when East End Park had been requisitioned for use by the military.

In 2013, both the cricket and football clubs face a very uncertain future.

St. Mirren (Venus Cricket Club)

A group of young men formed Venus Cricket Club in 1874. A near neighbour of Kelburne Cricket Club and a precursor to Ferguslie Cricket Club, they required financial assistance to continue operating as a cricket club.

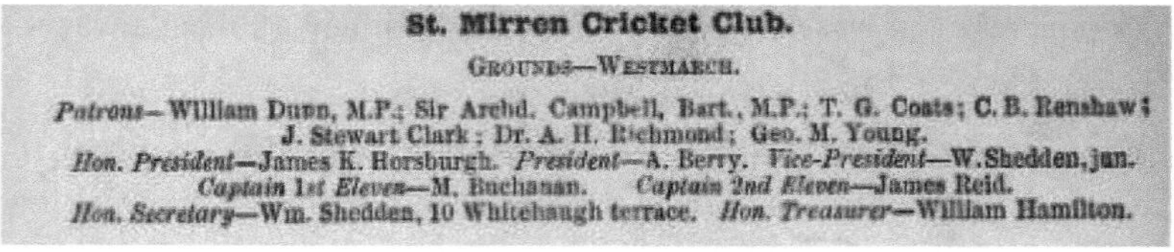

St. Mirren Cricket Club.

GROUNDS—WESTMARCH.

Patrons—William Dunn, M.P.; Sir Archd. Campbell, Bart., M.P.; T. G. Coats; C. B. Renshaw; J. Stewart Clark; Dr. A. H. Richmond; Geo. M. Young.
Hon. President—James K. Horsburgh. *President*—A. Berry. *Vice-President*—W. Shedden, jun.
Captain 1st Eleven—M. Buchanan. *Captain 2nd Eleven*—James Reid.
Hon. Secretary—Wm. Shedden, 10 Whitehaugh terrace. *Hon. Treasurer*—William Hamilton.

Representatives of the club approached a local businessman who financed them on the condition that they changed the club's name to reflect the local area. The men chose the name "St Mirren" after St Mirin, the town's patron saint. The club played cricket in the summer months and rugby football in the winter.

In 1877, a motion to play by association rules was agreed by the club and two members walked to Glasgow to buy a ball. Taking pity on the boys, the shopkeeper gave them their fare home, adding they were the first from Paisley to buy a ball from him.

With other local cricket clubs such as Kelburne and Ferguslie meeting the cricketing needs of Paisley, together with the professionalisation of association football and the creation of the first Scottish Football League in 1890, the interests of the cricket club slowly faded away into history and St. Mirren Football Club concentrated on its football.

In March 2013, St. Mirren Football Club wins the Scottish League Cup for the first time with a 3-2 victory over Heart of Midlothian in the final.

St. Mirren - a debt-free football club that has involved its community for its community to engage the club with a new stadium and training facilities, and a local businessman as its Chairman, a former Paisley cricketer.

VENUS

St. Mirren Football Club.

Instituted 1877.—Grounds, Westmarch.

Patrons—Sir A. C. Campbell, Bart., M.P. Col. Thomas Glen Coats. Major R. M. M'Kerrell. D. M'Farlane.
Hon. President—William Dunn, M.P. *President*—Alexander M'Kechnie.
Vice-President—Dr. Bruce. *Hon. Treasurer*—J. C. Hutcheson.
Hon. and Financial Secretary—Thomas Thomson, Craw road. *Match Secretary*—A. C. Gemmill, 17 Greenhill road. *Captain (1st Eleven)*—A. Brown. *Captain (2nd Eleven)*—J. M'Gregor.
Office - bearers elected in May annually.

West End Cricket Club—Instituted 1864.—The office-bearers for the year are as follows:—President, John Kerr, Esq., Trochrague and Heathfield; vice-president, Charles Lyle; secretary, James Montgomerie; treasurer, William Adams; captain, Daniel Kerr; committee, Robert Adam, Robert Kerr, J. L. M'Clure, and F. W. Shortridge. Ground, Bentinck Grounds. Annual subscription, £1 1s.

WEST END

NORTHERN

UNITED NORTHERN CRICKET CLUB.

Ground—Brighton Place, Copeland Road, Govan.

Formed in June, 1874. Patrons, Duke of Portland, Earl of Zetland, &c.; hon. president, James Leask, Burntisland; president, A. C. Wood; vice-president, J. H. Wilson; management committee, Messrs. A. C. Wood, J. H. Wilson, J. Sutherland, R. Brown, W. R. Danskin, Alex. Henderson, W. Robertson, A. Taylor, jun., and J. W. Wood; match committee, Messrs. Alex. Henderson, F. Houston, A. D. Nisbet, J. Hutcheson, and R. Brown; hon. treasurer, John Sutherland, 14 South Apsley Place; hon. secy., Robert Brown, 197 St. Vincent St., Glasgow.

Helensburgh

First formed as far back as 1874, Helensburgh were based for most of their existence at Ardencaple Park, the home of Helensburgh Cricket Club.

Football matches were played on what is now the present Helensburgh RFC's ground. Facilities were apparently very basic, with some terracing and a small pavilion while the pitch was usually a quagmire.

CRICKET.

Some years since by the munificence of Sir James Colquhoun and several gentlemen resident in Helensburgh, several acres of ground were set apart in the east end of Helensburgh as play-ground. A charter to the land was granted to the magistrates, and it has been enclosed and laid off for cricket, quoits, and kindred games. It is much frequented in the summer season. It is open to all without charge, and the habitual players have formed various clubs, admission to any of which can be obtained on the easiest terms. We have as yet no distinguished cricketers, the game having been but recently introduced; but the enthusiasm and zeal with which it is followed encourages a hope that a year or two hence some of the players will be able to distinguish themselves in friendly competition with older clubs.

Helensburgh Cricket Club.

Ground—Ardencaple Park.
President—Sir Jas. Colquhoun.
Captain — Harry T. Henderson.
Vice-Captains—H. C. Toppin and J. J. Halsey.
Secretary and Treasurer—J. Locke Anderson, Ava Lodge.
Match Secretary—H. C. Toppin.
Committee—A. B. Mitchell, C. E. Ball, W. H. Luther, Wm. M. Milne, J. F. Duncan, J. H. Sharp, A. Stewart, and T. Redpath.
Professional—Wm. Griffiths.

HELENSBURGH

Lomond Street, Possilpark.

Macfarlane, Walter, & Co.
Possilpark Football Club
Possilpark Cricket Club

POSSILPARK

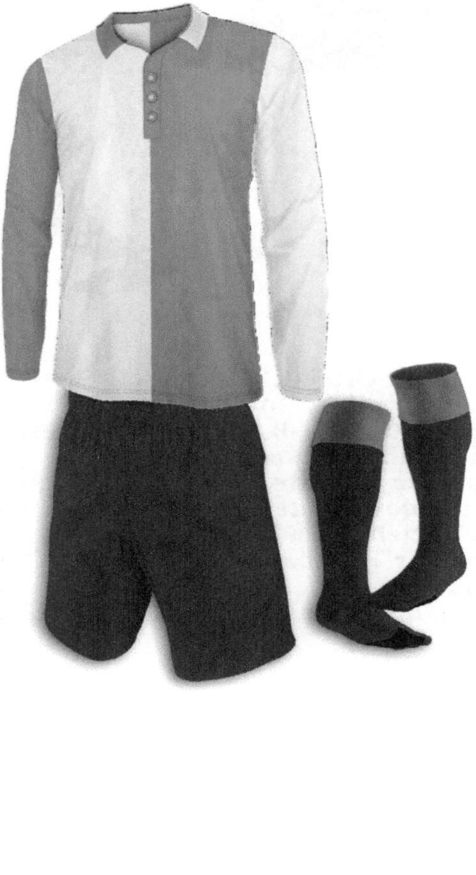

DRUMPELLIER

Drumpellier Cricket Club—Col. D. C. R. C. Buchanan, C.B. president & captain; Captain G. F. R. Colt, vice-president; David Crichton, sec. & treasurer

Drumpellier Estate Office, Drumpellier, Coatbridge—Frederick G. D. Bryan, factor; David Crichton, assistant factor

Drumpellier Football Club—Col. D. C. R. C. Buchanan, C.B. hon. president; John Foulds, hon. treasurer; William M'Intyre, hon. secretary [manager

WESTERN

WESTERN CRICKET CLUB.

Instituted 1862.

GROUND—KNIGHTSWOOD PARK, ANNISLAND TOLL.

Patrons—Marquis of Bute, Earl of Glasgow, Alex. Whitelaw, M.P., John Ross, jun., Esq., Colonel Buchanan of Drumpellier. President, Colonel Campbell of Blythswood; vice-president, A. W. Rattray of Callington Mains; hon. treasurer, James Steadman; hon. secretary, John D. More; committee, James Kelly, Geo. A. D. C. Ferguson, R. M. Liddell, W. H. A. Dalrymple, and W. Stewart; match committee, first eleven, W. Stewart, W. H. A. Dalrymple, and R. M. Liddell, secretary, 169 W. George Street; second eleven match committee, W. A. Dunlop, and J. Boyd, secretary. Annual subscription, £1 11s, 6d.

EAST-END CRICKET CLUB.

Instituted 1869.

GROUND—HELENVALE PARK, HIGH BELVIDERE.

Patrons—The Hon. the Lord Provost; Right Hon. the Earl of Glasgow; Dr. Chas. Cameron, M.P.; Alex. Whitelaw, M.P.; Bailie W. Collins; Councillor Finlay; Jas. A. Campbell, Esq.; John Matheson, jun., Esq.; Stephen Mason, Esq.; Daniel Burns, Esq.; president, John Mathie, M.D.; vice-president, James Wilson; secretary, Robert Farmer, 28 Tobago Street.

EAST END

Herriot, Arthur, jun., secretary for the Lancelot Cricket Club, 167 Græme street.

LANCELOT

UDDINGSTON

Meadowbank Park
1877 - 1893

St. Johnstone

St. Johnstone Football Club originated from the cricket club of the same name who were looking for a winter pastime and who had been kicking a ball around the ground for some time.

After many months of discussion, the football club was formed at a meeting on Tuesday 24th February 1885 and the first match played by St. Johnstone Football Club was two weeks later on Saturday 7th March 1885 when they defeated Caledonian 1-0.

Out of interest, with the fact that the St. Johnstone Cricket Club members played football prior to the official formation of the football club, 1884 continues to be shown as the year of formation on the club crest.

South Inch Mar-Aug 1885,
St Johnstone Recreation Grounds Aug 1885-Dec 1924,
Muirton Park 1924-Aug 1989,
McDermid Park Aug 1989-

ST. JOHNSTONE

Maroon shirts and white shorts 1884-1887,
White shirts and blue shorts 1887-88,
Red shirts and white shorts 1888-1894

First Lanarkshire Volunteer Rifles

First Lanarkshire Volunteer Rifles also played at Burnbank between 1874 and 1879 and the last reference that I can find for the team is in 1883. The founding father of the First Lanarkshire Volunteer Rifles militia was a Lt-Colonel HE Crum-Ewing.

Burnbank was used for sports, parades and drill practices. The formation of the cricket club, along with the football team, is listed in the Cricket Scotland historical archives as 1874.

Lt-Colonel HE Crum-Ewing went on to become the first president of the Glasgow Academicals Club and can be in some way considered responsible for the various ground and building relocations associated with Glasgow Academy and its educational and sporting interests.

The First Lanarkshire Volunteer Rifles football strip bears a striking resemblance to the colours used by Glasgow Academical school children for rugby today.

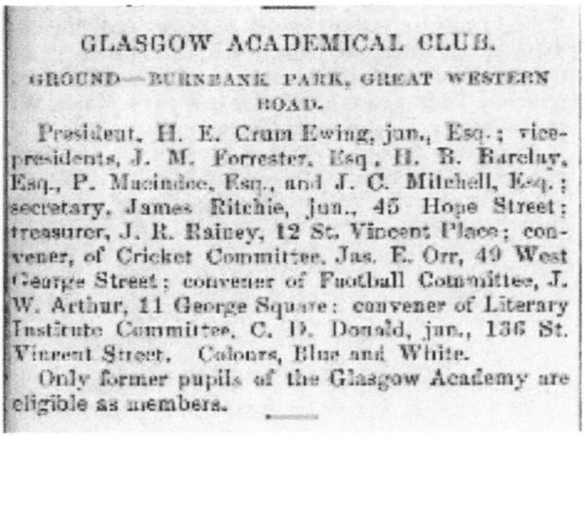

GLASGOW ACADEMICAL CLUB.

GROUND—BURNBANK PARK, GREAT WESTERN ROAD.

President, H. E. Crum Ewing, jun., Esq.; vice-presidents, J. M. Forrester, Esq., H. R. Barclay, Esq., P. Macindoe, Esq., and J. C. Mitchell, Esq.; secretary, James Ritchie, jun., 45 Hope Street; treasurer, J. R. Rainey, 12 St. Vincent Place; convener, of Cricket Committee, Jas. E. Orr, 49 West George Street; convener of Football Committee, J. W. Arthur, 11 George Square; convener of Literary Institute Committee, C. D. Donald, jun., 136 St. Vincent Street. Colours, Blue and White.

Only former pupils of the Glasgow Academy are eligible as members.

Rangers

Rangers Football Club was founded in 1872, playing their early games at Fleshers' Haugh on Glasgow Green. In 1875 the club moved briefly to Burnbank off Great Western Road and then in 1876 to Kinning Park, to the ground previously occupied by the Clydesdale Cricket Club, who had moved to Titwood.

The season of 1876-77 saw Rangers reach the Scottish Cup Final by way of victories over Queen's Park Juniors, Towerhill, Mauchline, Lennox and two byes, in the 3rd round and the semi-final. Their opponents were Vale of Leven, a more experienced team who had already made history by knocking out Queen's Park, winners of the trophy on every occasion so far. The final and first replay was held at Hamilton Crescent, Partick, resulting in 0-0 and 1-1 draws respectively. In the second replay, before a massive crowd of 8,000, Vale of Leven won 3-2.

RANGERS

Third Lanark

After the inaugural international between Scotland and England in 1872, a meeting was held later in the same year in December, at which the members of the 3rd Lanarkshire Rifle Volunteers, with the support of their commanding officer, Lt-Colonel HE Crum-Ewing, resolved to form a football club carrying the name of the regiment. It was then agreed to adopt "Guernseys" which were coarse knitted woolen tops with crew necks in regimental red, navy knickerbockers and hose. The team played on the regimental drill ground off Victoria Road at Inglefield Park in before moving into the first Cathkin Park in Cathcart Road in 1875.

The first playing field of the team was the Regimental drill ground at Victoria Road, Glasgow which was situated just to the south of the Regimental Headquarters, with occasional indoor training at Regimental drill hall in Coplaw Street, Govanhill, before ultimately moving to a 'new' ground, Old Cathkin Park in 1875.

The ground was offered to the team by the then owners 'Dixons' which was a well known ironworks in Cathcart Road, Glasgow and after making the surface playable goalposts and crossbars (as opposed to tapes) were erected. A grandstand was built in 1878 with the ultimate accolade coming, for all the subsequent hard work carried out in developing the ground, when in 1884 Old Cathkin Park was chosen as the venue for the then annual Scotland v England match resulting in a 1-0 win for Scotland which was their 5th win in a row against the 'Auld Enemy'.

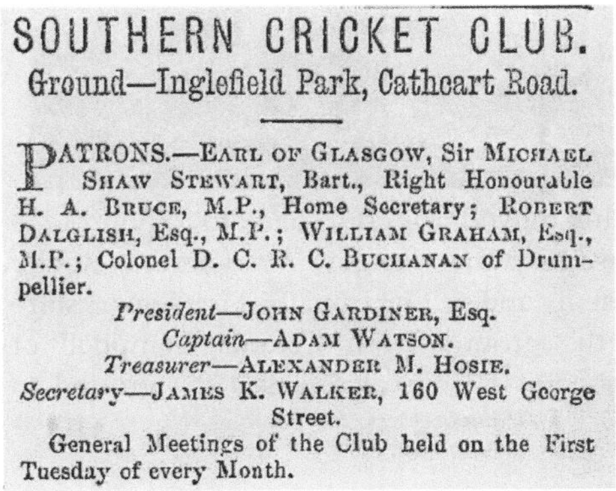

SOUTHERN CRICKET CLUB.
Ground—Inglefield Park, Cathcart Road.

PATRONS.—Earl of Glasgow, Sir Michael Shaw Stewart, Bart., Right Honourable H. A. Bruce, M.P., Home Secretary; Robert Dalglish, Esq., M.P.; William Graham, Esq., M.P.; Colonel D. C. R. C. Buchanan of Drumpellier.

President—John Gardiner, Esq.
Captain—Adam Watson.
Treasurer—Alexander M. Hosie.
Secretary—James K. Walker, 160 West George Street.

General Meetings of the Club held on the First Tuesday of every Month.

Caledonian

According to the Cricket Scotland archives, Caledonian Cricket Club was founded in 1850 and the football team was formed in 1875. Caledonian Cricket Club played at Holyrood Park, Burnbank and Kelvinbridge and hosted matches against local clubs and English touring sides.

CALEDONIAN CRICKET CLUB.
Instituted 1852.
GROUND—HOLYROOD PARK, NEW CITY ROAD.

H. E. C. Ewing, jun., president; James Watson, jun., 3 Windsor Terrace, secretary; G. H. Hutton, treasurer; John Campbell, John Gardner, Neale Thomson, Robert Hutchison, Thomas Orr, council; John Gardner, Robert Patterson, Robert Hutchison, match committee. Members, eighty. Annual subscription for ordinary members, £1 11s. 6d.; honorary members, £1. The monthly meetings of the club take place on the first Tuesday of each month in the club house, Holyrood Park.

Holyrood Park was at the beginning of the New City Road on the site of the Stow College. They moved to Burnbank, situated south of Great Western Road near to Dunearn Street and Woodlands Drive. The ground features in the photograph below, the tall spire is St. Mary's Cathedral, at the corner of Great Western Road and Napiershall Street.

When the Caledonian Cricket Club moved from Burnbank to Kelvinbridge in 1866, Burnbank was then used by the Glasgow Academicals Rugby Football Club and Glasgow Academy and sub-let from the First Lanarkshire Volunteer Rifles who leased the ground from Colonel Campbell of Blythswood, who, for one season in 1875-76, also leased the ground to Rangers.

Further research suggests that the Caledonian Cricket Club went defunct as a result of the Glasgow Academy moving from Elmbank Street in 1878 to where their ground once stood at Kelvinbridge.

Cricket was an incredibly well organised club structure long before rugby or football and a local example would be the fact that the forming of the West of Scotland Cricket Club in 1862 predated the forming of West of Scotland Rugby Football Club in 1865, so it is possible to surmise, that in its latter years, the Caledonian Football Club aspect continued with an influx of cricketers from local clubs wishing to play football during the winter months.

CALEDONIAN

Clydesdale Cricket Club v Caledonian 15th June 1867

CLYDESDALE V. CALEDONIAN

This match was played on Saturday last, on Kinning Park, and resulted in favour of the Clydesdale by 96 runs.

Owing to the long scoring on both sides only one innings could be played.

Score : -

CALEDONIAN		CLYDESDALE	
Russell, c and b A.Campbell	10	Macpherson, c Orr b N.Thomson	10
Hutchison, b Campbell	8	D.Duff, b Chalmers	77
W.Gardner, b D.Duff	4	C.Campbell, c Gardner, b Thomson	0
Laurence, c McPherson, b D. Duff	15	K.MacDonald, c Laurence, b Chalmers	16
Chalmers, b. D.Duff	19	J.McArly, b Hope	13
A.Hope, c McAllister, b D. Duff	0	J.Smith, run out	5
R.Patterson, b D.Duff	6	.J.Grant, c Orr, b Thomson	25
T.W.Orr, b D.Duff	7	McAllister, b Laurence	1
C.Thomson, b McPherson	29	J.Duff, lbw, b N.Thomson	3
Carrick, not out	5	E.Hendry, not out	23
N.Thomson, b McPherson	0	A.Campbell, c Orr, b Paterson	14
Byes, &c	5	Byes, &c	17
Total	108	Total	204

Umpires -Pierce and McKenzie.

Lenzie

Lenzie Cricket Club was formed in 1868. An association football team was formed by the cricketers in 1875 for winter exercise and played until disbanding in 1889.

They participated in the Scottish Cup until the 1886-87 season when they lost 13-0 at home to Vale of Leven.

In 1888, enthusiastic members formed a tennis section and became Lenzie Cricket and Tennis Club. The first AGM of the merged club listed 30 Lady Members and 40 Gentlemen Members. The committee was all male, but a Ladies' Committee provided teas at the club.

Lenzie Football Field to 1888, Middlemuir Park and Craigmillar Park 1888-89

In 1879, Lenzie Cricket Club became missionaries of association football when they played a demonstration game at the Ulster Cricket Ground against a team of local enthusiasts in one of the earliest competitive football matches to be held in what is now Northern Ireland.

Lennox

Lennox Cricket Club was to be found in Lennoxtown, north of Glasgow, and played at Levengrove Park. The cricket club started in 1867 and folded in May 1986. The cricketers turned to football as a sport for the winter months and ran a football section from 1873 until 1882.

In May 1986, I played for Lennox Cricket Club in their last ever game, a cup match against Kelvinside Academicals at Balgray. If Lennox had won this game, they would have continued on playing for the rest of that season, but alas it was not to be. Kelvinside Academicals folded themselves, a few seasons later.

Kirkintilloch

Kirkintilloch Cricket Club was founded in 1862. Again, the cricketers turned to association football as a means of keeping fit during the winter months and ran a football team from 1876 to 1881.

Hamilton

HAMILTON

Formed April 1874, disbanded April 1879.

Connected to Hamilton Cricket Club.

Cricket & Football was played by this club, first of all at South Haugh and then South Avenue 1874-1879.

Stenhousemuir

Stenhousemuir Cricket Club operated a football team out of The Tryst from 1884-1886. They played in red and blue striped shirts & dark blue shorts

STENHOUSEMUIR

Southern

Southern Cricket Club ran a football team out of Inglefield Park from 1872-1880

SOUTHERN

East Stirlingshire (Bainsford Bluebonnets Cricket Club)

East Stirlingshire was formed as a cricket club in 1868. The club is thought to have been originally formed as an off-shoot of the Bainsford Bluebonnets Cricket Club, who themselves created an association football section known as Bainsford Britannia in 1880. A year later, relations turned sour between the sections and the football broke away from their parent club and re-emerged as East Stirlingshire Football Club.

An interesting aspect to consider in the history of the East Stirlingshire/ Bainsford Bluebonnets/Bainsford Brittannia saga is that the club was to be found in the village of Bainsford near to Falkirk.

The locale of what was once the village of Bainsford is between the River Carron and the Forth and Clyde Canal and until the early 1900s, a bascule bridge across the canal was to be found there.

Falkirk Cricket Club - 1882-1886
Dark blue shirts, white shorts, red stockings.

FALKIRK

The cricket ground was called Randyford Park and another local football team, namely Falkirk who were founded in 1876, used this cricket ground in the winter months for its home games from 1878 until 1880. Falkirk's first ever competitive game was played here in the Scottish Cup in 1878 when they beat Campsie Glen 1-0. Peversely, Bainsford Britannia's first ever football match was against Falkirk's second eleven who beat them 7-0.

Balclutha

Formed in September 1885 by members of the Balclutha Cricket Club, who operated out of Ladyburn Park in Greenock

The Shearing of the Willow

As my investigations progressed, it suddenly became apparent that the majority of the cricket clubs in the Glasgow area started to suddenly disappear from around 1878 to about 1890. A great number of them had simply folded as the land that they used to play on was swallowed up by Glasgow's continuous expansion as a city, but there had to be other factors or reasons for so many clubs to just simply die in such a relatively short space of time.

The importance of these clubs cannot be allowed to be forgotten. Collectively, they were responsible for the shaping of the many social and sporting relationships that we now take for granted. These cricket clubs, their patrons and their members, were the exploratory front-line foot soldiers whose actions created the recreational structures that exist today.

I had to find something contemporaneous that would describe the shifting landscape of society in 1890. Having spent many hours of research and fruitless trips up the many dead-end streets of the internet, I finally stumbled upon a book called "Scottish Football Reminiscences and Sketches 1890" written by a chap called David Drummond Bone.

The book itself gives the reader a snapshot of football, its politics, its characters and a resume of some of the numerous reasons for the acceleration of the sport in the eighteen short years from 1872 and the first football international. One particular chapter answered many questions that I had:

Project Gutenberg - Scottish Football Reminiscences and Sketches 1890.

Author: David Drummond Bone

Chapter VI.—How Clubs were Started Long Ago

When the summer game of cricket was far more extensively played in Glasgow and District than it is now, those who understood the feelings and aspirations of young men engaged in it repeatedly considered the question in all its aspects, and a combination of circumstances have occurred within the last decade which had seriously affected that game.

The City of Glasgow could not, of course, afford to remain in a stationary condition to suit the convenience of a few thousands of cricketers. New streets had to be formed, new houses built all round, and with this advance upon civilisation came the deadly blow to cricket—at least juvenile cricket—and those clubs soon disappeared from the field. Ground after ground was swallowed up, and on the scene of many a hot and exciting match blocks of houses, railway stations, churches, and public works may now be seen. The Scotch youth, and for that part of it (just to give the sentence greater weight), the British youth, loves some kind of manly sport. Cricket he could no longer play for want of good and level ground, but then there was another game which, at least, could be played or learned under easy circumstances, even on a quiet street or big "free coup," and that was Association football.

They soon took to it kindly, and many of them struggled hard and procured a ground. Not one, of course, like that on which they used to have their cricket matches long ago, but one on which Farmer Lyon grazed his cows and sheep, and they had it for a trifle. What did they care about ridges and furrows, or that it was a difficult matter to see the lower goal-posts when you were at the east end? Not a straw. The only matter which annoyed them (and this only happened occasionally) was Lyon's bull. Their club colours were red jerseys, with a small white stripe, and "Jock" (that was the animal's name), used to scatter the lads about on the Friday evenings when they were engaged in a big side. The players generally managed to clear out in time, but the infuriated animal once goared the best ball the club had, and next morning, as they had to play the "Invincible" of Glasgow Green, a subscription had to be raised for a new one.

Football can thus be played under much more favourable conditions than cricket, or almost any other out-door game, at less expense, and this, in a great measure at least, is the secret of its popularity amongst the masses. It can also be played under nearly every condition of the atmosphere. Nothing seems to frighten the Scotch Association football player. Rain, hail, snow, and even frost, is treated with cool indifference. In England the ball is quietly laid aside with the advent of April and forgotten till the Autumn leaves are yellow and sear, but in Scotland Association football seems to have no recognised season at all, so far as the younger clubs and even a few of the seniors are concerned. With the sun making one's hair stick to his head with perspiration, and the thermometer at 90 degrees in the shade, they play away in the summer-time, and at Christmas attempt to dribble in half-a-foot of snow.

Meantime, the question about football being blotted out, can, I think, be easily answered in the negative, and upon these will depend the future prospect of Association Football in{72} Scotland. There are, in fact, "breakers ahead," and a strong and determined hand will have to take the wheel. The greatest of these is the "professional" football player, and the next the "greed of gate-money." "O! we never heard of a professional football player in Scotland," exclaims a chorus of voices; "there is no such thing. It's only in England." My remark, of course, is only beginning to be realised. The definition of professional in athletics "is one who runs (plays) for gain." Everybody knows what that means. If you receive any money whatever, directly or indirectly, from your club (except out of the private purses of the members), you are a professional. Are there not clubs, with great reputations, who have such members? If these are allowed to continue on the club books simply because they are good players, the committee are doing a great injustice to the other members, it may be under a mistaken notion. Now, as football has always been looked upon as a purely amateur game, and played by young men for their own amusement, it is to be hoped that the day is far distant when the professional football player, or even worse, the professional football "loafer," who does not work, but preys upon his fellow-members, will appear in a general form. In all conscience, if the public wish to see professional football (and I know from experience they don't), what would they think of the All-Scotland Eleven against the Champion Eleven of England?

That might sound all right, but with the recollection of how professional athletics of all kinds (with the remarkable exception of cricket) are now conducted, and their low associations, woe betide football when the professional element is introduced. It will assuredly be the signal for its decline and fall. As for the greed of gate-money, of which some clubs are so fond, much might be said. When I refer to the clubs who try to gather as much cash as they can during the season in order to pay their legitimate obligations and meet the heavy item of ground rent, I show up an honourable example, and one worthy of imitation; but when I hear of clubs who have gathered ten, yea twenty times more than is required for such purposes, and even get handsome donations besides from their patrons, deep in debt at the end of the season, I begin to wonder where all the money has gone.

I ask a young gentleman who has only lately become a member, and he tells me he knows nothing about the finance committee, but throws out grave hints about sordid motives and bare-faced applications for pecuniary assistance. In this respect clubs must be above suspicion, if they want the delightful game to hold its own and prosper. As a quid pro quo for this vicious practice, however, there is no game whose players are so charitable as those connected with Association Football. There is not a club in the Association that is not ready to play a "Charity Match," and far more has been given to the funds of charitable institutions by the actions of Association football clubs than all the other games in Scotland put together.

David Drummond Bone's commentary in this chapter does bring a wry smile to the face of someone who is deeply cynical and jaundiced about the true intentions of the movement of players around various Scottish cricket clubs in the 21st Century, but importantly, Bone provides an eye-witness testimony of what were the concerns of the day.

Armed with some of the information that David Drummond Bone's book provides, the blank spaces of the background of "Big House" cricket from its creation to its demise can now be painted in, along with the various scenery changes of a fifty year period.

Before the 1870s, most "Big House" estates encompassed many acres, with tenanted farms and villages under the feu of the owner. Most of these estates were well run ventures and sufficiently profitable to enable the owners to maintain other properties and also fund other projects and interests. While the Industrial Revolution undoubtedly created great wealth for those that owned the land, the same land had to be worked and developed, and the building of housing and the provision of utilities for a rising population all had an effect.

But as more and more land was being sold for "development" in a new modern age, an agricultural depression in the 1870s had a huge impact on the landowners themselves. Glasgow also suffered from an unexpected financial crisis. The city's wealth had a boom period between 1869 and 1877 and enjoyed unprecedented prosperity, however, prices became inflated in property, coal, iron and other raw materials, and with a growing saturation of a commodity driven industrial market, difficulties in financial circles were about to create a cataclysmic earthquake of such magnitude in the late 19th Century that the after-shock tremors are still being felt in the 21st Century.

The Shearing of the Willow – The Greed of Man

The City of Glasgow Bank, founded in 1839, was favoured by small investors who received reasonable dividends for their investments. The bank expanded as Glasgow enjoyed its place at the hub of the Industrial Revolution.

By 1877, there were 133 branches with many of them open in evenings to receive deposits. However, in October of that year, a deficit of £7,000 had been uncovered and the bank's operations were suspended for a two month period while investigations were made. With the agreement of other Scottish banks, trading resumed in 1878 and the deficit had been written off as nothing more than a glip.

In October 1878, the directors of the City of Glasgow Bank announced its immediate closure with liabilities of over £6m along with extensive loans with poor security and speculative investments in farming, mining and railway shares.

There had even been false reporting of its holdings and the balance sheets had all been falsified. The bank's share prices had also been kept deliberately high by the bank making secret purchases of its own stock. Such was the level of the deception by its directors, the failure of the bank and its subsequent bankruptcy caused hundreds of Glasgow businesses to collapse.

Nearly 1,600 of the bank's 1,819 shareholders were instantly ruined as their liability was not limited. The directors were all tried at the High Court in Edinburgh in January 1879, were all found guilty and sentenced to terms of imprisonment.

To explain the financial scale of the collapse of The City of Glasgow Bank, £7,000 in 1877 is the equivalent of £500,000 in 2012. Likewise, £6m would be worth over £500million at 2012 prices.

A déjà vu comparison can be made with the bank run that Northern Rock experienced in 2007 and the subsequent fallout it had on the British economy and beyond. The ripples of financial instability are still relentlessly lapping at the shores of our daily life and will do so for many years to come.

The Shearing of the Willow – The Impact on the World

The collapse of the City of Glasgow Bank had huge ramifications on the every day lives of ordinary people. Like the scourge of a plague, its victims were not exclusive or singular to any particular class or distinction. This crisis affected the rich, the poor, the healthy, the ill and the comfortable. The failure of the City of Glasgow Bank was a disaster for Scotland, its people, its trade and industry and all that had been achieved or contributed to was now at risk. Very few families escaped the effects of the Bank's collapse, if not within their immediate family circle, certainly through a close relative, friend or associate.

When the City of Glasgow Bank released its shareholder listings in June 1878, together with details of all its stocks and shares portfolios, newspapers all around the world, albeit mainly those of the Empire colonial territories and the United States, published them for reference.

The publication of the Bank's shareholder details and financial information was to enable the authorisation of a specific type of letter of credit, in which, a buyer extends an unsecured loan to a seller. This action was, and still is, referred to as a Red Clause Letter of Credit. This agreement enables the holder, who usually acts as a purchasing agent for buyers in another country, to receive funds for any merchandise outlined in the terms of the letter of credit.

The funds provided by the terms of a Red Clause Letter of Credit are known as advances. These advances are then deductable from the face amount of the Letter of Credit when Bills of Exchange are presented for payment. Red

Clause Letters of Credit are usually employed to facilitate international exports and trade, and are so known because particular parts are typed in red ink.

In layman terms, a Red Clause Letter of Credit in 1878 allowed suppliers around the world to be paid for their products or goods. These products or goods would normally be linked to wool and sheep farming, timber and raw materials. The supplier delivered his products or goods to the agent, who, once satisfied that all was correct, would call upon the Red Clause Letter of Credit at an overseas bank, and present the Bill of Exchange together with the Bills of Lading for export. This would allow the agent to be paid, who, in turn, would pay the supplier.

A Bill of Lading enabled merchants to know what had been loaded onto ships, issued signed receipts to certify the loading of products or goods on to vessels and to verify the condition of those products or goods at the time of loading. With the growth of mercantilism, Bills of Lading had become the documents of entitlement to the products or goods.

Whoever held the Bills of Lading could collect the goods at the dockside.

In the colonies and elsewhere, huge loans had been made to borrowers on inadequate security. Vastly speculative investments had been made by the City of Glasgow Bank in land, sheep farms and wool in New Zealand and Australia in the hope of recovering losses that the bank had made investing in mining stocks and American railway bonds and shares. The bank had made false reports to the fiscal officers concerning the amount of gold held as security for notes issued, and as the need for greater mis-statement arose, the extent of the falsification increased.

The last balance sheet published before the closure of the City of Glasgow Bank was dated 5th June 1878 and it indicated capital, reserves and undistributed profits totalling £1.6m.

Initial examinations by accountants, made immediately after the closure of the Bank, some four months later, revealed that the Bank's capital and reserves were entirely wiped out and the capital deficiency was estimated at the astounding figure of £6million, which converts as £500million in 2012. Red Clause Letters of Credit, Bills of Exchange and promissory notes had been drawn all around the world and the time delay of the notification of the City of Glasgow Bank's collapse would take time to be publically known overseas.

STOCKHOLDERS OF CITY OF GLASGOW BANK.

The following is a copy of the official list of persons holding stock in the City of Glasgow Bank on the 17th day of July, 1878, and of persons who have held stock therein at any time during the year immediately preceding the said 17th day of July, 1878, showing their names and addresses, and an account of the stock so held, as registered at the office of the Registrar of Joint-Stock Companies for Scotland.

The figures marked *a* relate to "additional stock held by existing stockholders during preceding year." The figures marked *b* are these entered in the column of the account of "stock held by persons no longer shareholders."

In distant Australia and New Zealand, the list of Stockholders of the City of Glasgow Bank was only published in the press in mid to late November 1878, some six weeks after the collapse. The knock-on effect of the disaster was to have grave consequences for supply, demand and payment of products and goods all around the world, and placed many into destitution and poverty.

The list of stockholders was published in Page 2 of the Otago Daily Times in New Zealand in Issue 5236 on 28th November 1878, nearly two months after the collapse.

The basics of Glasgow's rise as the Second City of the Empire through its trade via import and export was in jeopardy as a result of a fraud committed by a handful of individuals working within a bank.

In the Americas, the waves of the collapsed Bank broke on the eastern sea-board. At its liquidation, the City of Glasgow Bank owned, among other American assets, securities of the Western Union Railroad Company, which connected Lake Michigan and the Mississippi River, the Racine Warehouse and Dock Company, considerable stock in the Chicago, Milwaukee & St. Paul Railway Company along with other companies, land and mortgages. The American security holdings of the City of Glasgow Bank consisted of $407,300 in Chicago, Milwaukee & St. Paul stock, $2,926,000 in bonds and $1,992,340 in stock of the Western Union, and $300,000 in Racine Warehouse and Dock, plus $44,810 owed by the Western Union Railroad Company. When totalled together and converted into comparative Sterling terms of 2012, the sum is around £450million alone.

This was not a financial crisis that was contained to Scotland. This was reverberating around the world. The effect of the bank's failure on Glasgow business had been immense with hundreds of Glasgow businesses folding as a result, and with it, the 1819 shareholders and their families suffered greatly. Indeed, the City of Glasgow Bank failure emphasised the desirability of the Scottish banks to accept the principle of limited liability to protect stockholders and within a few years of the failure, the banks resolved mutually to become limited.

The City of Glasgow Bank had been attractive to small depositors such as the common man, the working class and the artisans, and as such, the Bank had operated an extensive branch system that opened in the evenings and paid high deposit rates to its customers.

Its failure resulted in greater publicity *"than had ever previously fallen to the lot of any business establishment"* and to quote the Edinburgh Courant of 22nd October 1878 where the plight of the shareholders and the depositors was summed up in a single sentence *"It will long be remembered by thousands in Scotland as the saddest and darkest day in their history, in as much as it carried ruin and desolation into happy homes in almost every town and village in the country."*

Pulpits throughout the land thundered on Sunday 20th October 1878 as the principals in the case had strong Free Church connections. Over 40 church ministers were instantly ruined. Shops, businesses and trades closed and thousands of depositors could not gain access to their savings. Employees lost their jobs and the calamitous nature of the situation was profound. This one situation triggered a tsunami of financial destruction that few would be fortunate to initially survive, and those that did, had to dispose of assets to realise funds to offset the threat of bankruptcy or maintain the viability of their businesses, whatever they were.

Hunter, John, merchant, Glasgow - 3600
Hendry, Charles, 11 Royal Exchange Buildings, Glasgow - - 100
Houldsworth, Arthur Hooton, Springfield House, Lasswade - - 4000
Hunter, John, merchant, Carnock, by Dunfermline, in liferent, and Margaret Young Hunter and Helen Ford Hunter, his daughters, in fee - - 100
Hume, Peter, 5 Buchanan street, Glasgow - - - - 300
Harrington, James Paxton, warehouseman, Glasgow - - - 500
Hunter, Rev. Joseph, The Manse, Cockburnspath, Berwickshire - - 100
Hendry, Ebenezer, 54 Murray place, Stirling - - - - 100
Heddle, Miss Emily Margaret, Sudbrook Park, Petersham, near Richmond, Surrey - - - 100

Ebenezer Hendry, a former Clydesdale cricketer who had also played against Queen's Park in the first Association Football Cup Final, and also one of the founding committee members of the Scottish Football Association in 1873, was caught up in the collapse of the City of Glasgow Bank.

The last four months of 1878 were to become the worst four months of Ebenezer Hendry's life. On the 6th August 1878, his brother, Alexander, aged 29, committed suicide in Stirling; the reasons for doing so have never been discovered. Eight weeks later, on the 1st October 1878, the City of Glasgow Bank collapsed. Ebenezer Hendry held a £100.00 share that not only became worthless overnight, but that he, along with the rest of the shareholders would be held liable for £2,750.00 per £100.00 share held, a considerable amount of money, and when converted to 2012 prices equates as a debt of £218,300.00.

He was able to procure funds to stay solvent by borrowing from elsewhere, but he was lucky that he was able to do so. When the Bank affairs were settled in late 1882, he was one of only 254 out of the original 1819 shareholders to avoid bankruptcy.

On the 9th December 1878, his mother, Isabella Thomson, died at the age of 71. She had taken a stroke and had been paralysed for a month and one cannot help but wonder if the unfortunate suicide of one son and the financial disaster that had beset another were the contributory factors in her demise.

Ebenezer Hendry was able to survive the tragedies that befell him in 1878, and when you factor in that he was also married with 6 young children, the scale of what happened to the other small shareholders does make one appreciate that this had all been perpetuated by a handful committing fraud with complete disregard for the consequences for those that would be affected.

In a 21st Century context, bankruptcy and insolvency are unfortunately common enough occurrences for us all to encounter, however, in the late 19th Century, the stigma and shame attributable to bankruptcy automatically made the debtor an instant social pariah and ultimately impacted on family life and social standing.

The Houldsworths were an extended Southron family (moved to Scotland) who bustled their way to prominence through the crowd of native competition. They were successful cotton spinners, machinery makers, iron founders, and iron masters in Lanarkshire and in Ayrshire and became major players in the industrialisation of the Glasgow area and provided mass employment to the populace in a great many ventures. The family had made fortunate purchases of land and estates, such as Woodside, Anderston, Belvedere and Cranstonhill that would be eventually built upon and covered with streets to form parts of the layout of the City of Glasgow we know today. The Messrs Houldsworth enjoyed connections and patronages at a number of the early cricket clubs such as Ayr and West of Scotland, and are, in no small way, important to acknowledge for what they originally contributed to and created in Scotland's ignored sporting heritage.

For one of them, Arthur Hooton Houldsworth, acknowledgement and remembrance, would not be for the Scottish cricketing legacies that he was a part of, but for an important piece of Scottish civil litigation and a ruling that is still extremely relevant all over the world nearly 140 years since raising it.

Arthur Hooton Houldsworth, who was born in Manchester on the 11th July 1847, had found his business interests had been seriously compromised by the collapse of the City of Glasgow Bank. In February 1877, he had purchased £4000.00 of consolidated stock from the City of Glasgow Bank. As a stockholder, Houldsworth was going to be personally liable for £111,000.00, which in 2012 terms equates as £8,732,000.00. On 21st December 1878, he raised at the Court of Session in Edinburgh, an action by a Shareholder against the Company in Liquidation (The City of Glasgow Bank) for Damage caused by Fraudulent Misrepresentations of Directors inducing him to purchase Shares.

The craves of the action were:

(1) for payment of "£9046, 5s. 3d., being the loss and damage originally sustained by the pursuer by and through his purchase from the defenders, the said City of Glasgow Bank, of £4000 consolidated stock of the said company, at a price of £9000 sterling, £46, 5s. 3d. of stamp-duty and fee:"

(2) for decree ordaining the defenders "to free and relieve the pursuer of £20,000 sterling, being the further loss and damage sustained by him by and through the first call in the liquidation upon the said stock;"

(3) for payment to the pursuer of £200,000, or such other sum as shall be ascertained by our said Lords in the process to follow hereon to be the loss and damage sustained, or to be sustained, by the pursuer, by and though the further calls to be made in the said liquidation; or otherwise, that the defenders should be ordained to relieve the pursuer of such further calls as the same may fall due, besides making payment of the sums concluded for

in respect of damage already accrued."

Houldsworth had raised the action in an attempt to recover his original investment and sought damages and compensation for being fraudulently induced into buying stock in the City of Glasgow Bank.

The case was heard in court and the judgement assoilzied the defenders. An appeal was lodged and was subsequently dismissed with the ruling that, in Houldsworth's case (Houldsworth v City of Glasgow Bank (1880) 5 App Cas 317), he being a subscribing shareholder, he therefore cannot recover damages from the company for fraudulent misrepresentation in connection with the subscription for the shares. The shareholder's only remedy would be to seek rescission of the contract of allotment of shares, which would remove his name from the shareholders' register of members, and thereby to receive restitution of his application money.

This ruling in the Houldsworth case protected creditors, as it maintains the capital of a company by preventing a shareholder, whether directly or indirectly, from receiving back any part of the shareholder's contribution to the capital of the company and also prevented a person who is a shareholder from claiming a debt, or making a claim, against the company in that person's capacity as a shareholder of the company, if payments of the debt or claim will directly or indirectly recoup the money subscribed by the shareholder for the shares acquired by it.

This ruling is now an integral element of company law, not only in Scotland and the United Kingdom, but in Australia, New Zealand, Singapore, Malaysia, Indonesia, India, the Americas and the West Indies. Today, it regularly features as a point of reference in court actions taking place all over the world.

The collapse of the City of Glasgow Bank had rocked the world and affected many, whether it be the poor and destitute, the working classes, the ordinary man, the clergy, the middle and upper classes, businesses, small traders, investors, large concerns, industry, commerce, trade and mercantilism, finance and banking, the privileged, landed gentry and aristocracy. The repercussions would determine the changes in society for the rest of the 19th Century and beyond, and we still feel them and we still do not look to the past for the answers to the future.

In Scotland, the changes to society were rapid. While many estates were just able to sustain themselves, by 1880 the agricultural depression and the collapse of The City of Glasgow Bank placed many of them into extreme financial difficulties while attempting to balance their income versus expenditure. There was no more spare land to sell off for progress as the apex of the parabola of the Industrial Revolution had been reached. The zenith had been attained and it was now going to be a downhill journey towards its nadir. From herein, there had to be a consolidation of the expansion. For many of the "Big Houses", their successful enterprises and land management ethics where communities were created, engaged and provided for in the expectancy that these same communities would engage the "Big House" would prove to be their downfall. The land of these estates, and what was on them, was now up for sale.

For many of the "Big House" owners, the short term solution to recover from unexpected financial difficulty was to simply sell off parts of their estates to those that wished to buy. Many estates were bought and subsequently turned into plots, and a good example of this practice was the Stobcross estate where a syndicate purchased it for £3,750.00. Portions of the Stobcross estate fetched between £3.00 to £5.00 per square yard and at a price of £5.00 per square yard, the whole sixty acres yielded a return of about £3.5 million for the syndicate.

Development that began in Glasgow's west end led to an increase in the demand for houses and speculative builders were always eager to supply a ready market. The playing fields along Great Western Road, once the venues of cricket, rugby and football matches, were no more. The expansive 18 acres of Burnbank were sold off and tenements were built to varying standards where some had the external appearance of luxurious terraced houses, while others, designed for artisans and their families, were more utilitarian in style.

Similarly, the fields and estates of areas of Glasgow such as Dennistoun and Govanhill saw densities of handsome middle-class tenements constructed and Shawlands, Pollokshaws, Langside and Cathcart saw the creation of numerous tenement blocks on what had been fields, exhausted mine-workings and green spaces.

David Drummond Bone comments on this situation, but doesn't enter into specifics. You are left with an opinion that he is desperately trying to tell the reader something, but, probably as a result of the circumstances, sensitivities and politics of the time, he cannot, and writes his thoughts in a cryptic manner. It has taken over 120 years for the cipher to be found to de-code the message inside his chapter, but now found, the true intent of his piece is revealed and he insinuates that the advent of professional football will damage that sport in the way that ruthless mercenary expediency had almost killed off cricket, the clubs and the resultant loss of the grounds.

The "Big House" land-owners had not only controlled their estates but the people living on them. Very few in the community could vote, and those that did tended to be the owner's friends, approved tradesmen, senior employees or valued tenants. The man in the "Big House", more often than not, owned a voter's home, was his employer or allowed them to operate a trade on his land, and subsequently, the voters did not challenge the local candidate who usually was the man in the "Big House". Social changes in the 1870s and 1880s led to electoral reform which then entitled over 60% of the male population to vote. Re-alignment of constituency boundaries led to candidates, who had enjoyed many years without opposition, now faced with an electorate outside of his influence or control. The power of the "Big House" owners was slowly being diminished and was curtailed further with the creation of local authorities.

The parliamentary reforms of the late 1890s and early 1900s finally ended the influence of the "Big Houses" upon their communities and with it, the necessity of "Big House" cricket died. Over a 50 year period, the novelty of furtherance by networks and opportunity had been replaced with a new option, and a simple one at that, and it was the freedom of choice.

Such was the unexpected growth, development and expansion created by the Industrial Revolution in the Glasgow area, where an agricultural society was transformed into an all-devouring industrialised leviathan over a relatively short period of time, and then was abruptly interrupted by a chain of unexpected events, I cannot help myself but make a comparison of its effect with classical history and the exploits of Alexander the Great.

On succession to the throne of Macedonia at the age of 19, Alexander went on a pursuit of undefeated conquest of the then known world. This conquest was known as Hellenism and all nations, peoples, beliefs and practices fell under its spell. Hellenism paved the way for the spread of Christianity and other religions, academia, knowledge, commerce, trade and concepts that we all take for granted in the 21st Century, yet, on Alexander's death at the relatively young age of 33, as a result of a fever contracted in Babylon, and with the world entirely at his mercy, the juggernaut of Hellenistic expansion stopped and died with him, his dream was quartered by his generals and we live in a world determined by what they left behind.

As Plutarch remarked in the 'Life of Alexander':

"Such contentedness and change of view in regard to every kind of life does the infusion of reason bring about. When Alexander heard from Anaxarchus of the infinite number of worlds, he wept, and when his friends asked him what was the matter, he replied, "Is it not a matter for tears that, when the number of worlds is infinite, I have not conquered one?"

A Story with a Moral.

On searching the story of the collapse of the City of Glasgow Bank and the consequences that befell individuals, businesses, trade, institutions, sport and recreation and many other aspects of late Victorian era life, I came across a newspaper article of the time that explained some of the many realities that ordinary people faced.

The Maitland Mercury & Hunter River General Advertiser (NSW)
Thursday 16 December 1880

A little story of an instructive and a most interesting character is to be found hidden away among the dry columns of figures at page 59 of the Judicial Statistics of Scotland for the year 1879, which have just been issued. At that page is given a return of the number of persons in the various prisons of Scotland for civil debt at the end of the year, and the length of time during which some of them had been incarcerated. It appears from this return that upon 2d Sept., 1878, a person was thrown into the prison of Forfar for debt. Thirty days after he had been locked up the City of Glasgow Bank failed; and within three weeks thereafter the directors of the Bank were taken into custody on the charge of fraud. Five months after the 2nd September, 1878-that is, on 1st February, 1879, the Forfarshire debtor still being in prison, five of the directors of the Bank having been found guilty of fraud to the extent of some millions sterling, were sentenced, at the High Court of Justiciary, to eight months' imprisonment, and carried off to Ayr gaol to undergo the punishment imposed upon them for the crime which had spread ruin, accompanied by death and insanity in some cases, over the length and breadth of the land. On 1st October, 1879 (thirteen months after the 2nd September, 1878), the Forfarshire debtor still being in prison, the doors of the Ayr prison were thrown open for the liberation of the five directors, who had expiated their crime, so far as responsibility to man was concerned: and yet three months afterwards -31st December, 1879 - the date to which the returns come up, the debtor had not been liberated, and for anything we know he may be in prison still. Now the statistics do not condescend upon the exact amount for which this dreadful debtor was thrown into gaol; but they enable us to stale a sum beyond what his liabilities could not extend.

There were 21 debtors in the prison of Forfar at the end of last year, and with the exception of one whose debts were over £50 and under £100, none of their liabilities exceeded £50, and 13 of them had debts under £20. So that here was an individual, whose honesty, the public prosecutor did not feel warranted in challenging by preferring a criminal charge, suffering at least sixteen months' imprisonment for a debt not exceeding £100, without trial by judge or jury, and his liberty still at the mercy of the caprice of a single individual. Had he picked his creditor's pocket of the money, he certainly would not have been visited with any- thing like such a lengthened term of confinement, not being a previously-convicted thief; and at the end of his term his crime would have been purged: just as at the end of their eight mouths the City of Glasgow Bank Directors had purged their criminal squandering of £5,000,000 of their creditors' money.

But at the end of his sixteen months' confinement this debtor, instead of having purged his paltry obligation of £50 or so, had actually increased it by £25, the price paid by his creditors for punishing him. The contrast between the consequences brought upon individuals by a possibly honest obligation of a small amount on the one hand, and a certainly dishonest enormous obligation on the other, simply fills one with amazement that a state of the law so terribly unequal in its pressure was permitted to exist so long.

Locations Of The Clubs.

In the 21st century, we take many things for granted and very few of us ever wonder why certain buildings, facilities, parks, roads and railways are where they are. None of us ever really ask why that railway station is located at that particular place or what was the rationale behind the building of this or the placing of that.

It is very simple to explain – as Glasgow expanded as a result of the Industrial Revolution, more and more of its green space and surrounding countryside was swallowed up by for the necessity of progress.

In a sporting aspect, consider the following – the majority of bowling clubs, tennis clubs, golf courses and football and rugby grounds are close to railway lines, and in a Glasgow area context, cricket grounds. With pertinence to the cricket grounds, they were the original sporting facilities in Glasgow. They were the first in situ, and with travel access to them facilitated by the ever-growing rail infrastructure, commuting to and from them to play or watch cricket was a relatively easy affair.

As time has passed, many branches and stations of the rail infrastructure have gone, and similarly, many of the original cricket grounds and playing areas have disappeared, but both were there, although now lost through the continual redevelopment of Glasgow and its surrounding areas. If you look at the list of extant cricket clubs in the west of Scotland, they are beside or nearby current and former railway lines and stations of a rail infrastructure that was at some point the property of the Caledonia Railway Company.

By 1874, the south side was beginning to change. More and more residential properties were being built with the sandstone, quarried locally, being delivered by the railways. Schools, churches, hospitals and parks were constantly appearing. The urban development of Glasgow was relentless.

As a useless piece of information, the two types of sandstone that were used in Glasgow's construction were known as Glasgow Blonde sandstone and Giffnock sandstone, which is brown in colour. Unfortunately, both these types of sandstone can weather poorly if exposed to a highly polluted environment and discolour badly as well as showing signs of granular disintegration and scaling. For those readers of a certain age, they will remember that the majority of the sandstone buildings in Glasgow ended up having a black appearance as a result of smog, the weather and other airbourne pollutants. Most of the sandstone buildings retained this black appearance until the early 1970s, when a city-wide grant entitled sand-blasting initiative allowed for a comprehensive cleaning programme to begin that cleared a century's worth of grime from its edifices.

While there were still large tracts of land that belonged to various estates and concerns, and the multitude of fields and pastures, wooded areas, exhausted mine-workings and green spaces were interspersed with a sprinkling of occasional dwelling houses, hamlets and villages, a huge part of what was referred to as then as the south side of Glasgow, had been set aside and designated as recreational with the creation of what we now call the Queen's Park, complete with ponds, bandstands and playing fields.

This cartoon from the North British Daily Mail shows the newly created recreation grounds to be found at Queen's Park. In the distance, there is the flagpole at the highest point within the park. Top left of the picture has an outline of the Victoria Infirmary in the latter stages of its construction. A large number of football matches are taking place with spectators thronging the respective touchlines.

In the bottom left hand corner of the cartoon, a goal-keeper rests, almost nonchalantly, against his goal post, appearing to be oblivious to the berating that one of his team-mates is receiving about his performance on the pitch by an obviously incensed spectator.

A normal Glasgow Saturday afternoon and nothing has really changed.

Sometimes, clubs were moved location for the construction of the railway lines with Clydesdale being a perfect example. They were originally located in Kinning Park and were then moved elsewhere locally and were to be found to the west of the General Terminus Railway in Kinning Park. In 1874, Sir John Stirling Maxwell then advised Clydesdale they would have to move again and he offered them a new ground in Pollokshields called Titwood.

Clydesdale's move to Titwood was probably agreed because, although the surrounding area was still green fields, their new ground was beside a railway line, with an Act of Parliament in 1874 having decreed further rail construction to be commenced locally, thus bringing easier access to the club while being ideally placed as a recreational outlet, and with the expectancy of residential development scheduled to take place around them in the forthcoming years, all of this would lead to an increase of membership.

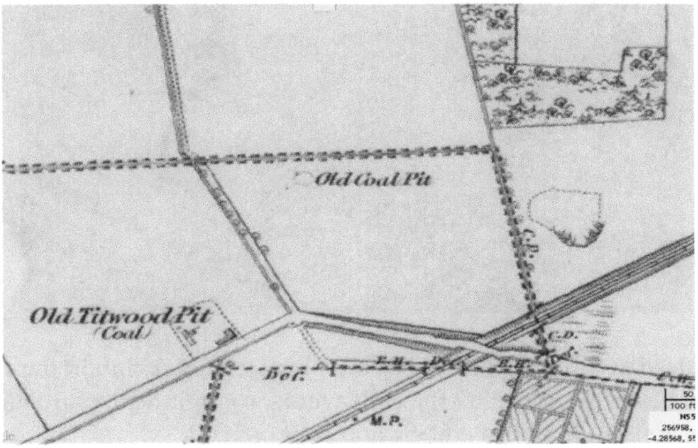

Clydesdale would be fortunate in that their move to Titwood, on land owned by Sir John Stirling Maxwell that had been previously worked for its yield of coal by William Dixon, was beside Crossmyloof Station and near to the proposed extension of the Cathcart Railway and two new stations of Maxwell Park and Pollokshields West and the laying out of streets and houses.

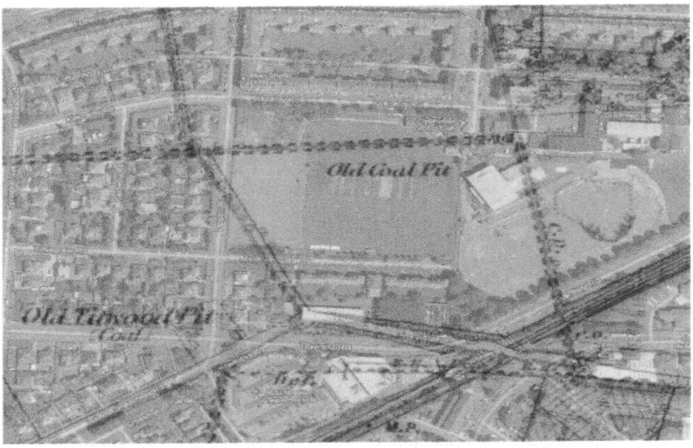

But Clydesdale's place as probably the premier cricket club in the west of Scotland has been earned by the endeavours, commitment, patronage and financial assistance of its members and supporters.

But that has not always been the case. Clydesdale's existence at Titwood comes from the benevolence of others financially prepared to assist the club, regardless of what their own motivation for doing so was for.

While conducting research in Glasgow's Mitchell Library, I unearthed a document whose content goes some way to confirm that the concept of "Big House" cricket, and its ideals, was not just a whimsical supposition but was an ethos that was very much alive and in practice.

140 years ago, the various cricketers and cricket clubs of Glasgow banded together to assist a fellow club. Clydesdale Cricket Club's then ground was required for urban development and expansion of the railway network,

and having secured a new venue at Titwood in Pollokshields, September 1875 would see the club play its last cricket matches at Kinning Park, with the football section playing its last games on the ground in March 1876. But Clydesdale's move to Titwood was problematic.

It had been the scene of extensive mine workings and it required a considerable amount of groundwork to turn it into a decent playing facility befitting the club's stature. For the development to begin, a sum of money was required, but that was something that Clydesdale Cricket Club did not possess.

Public subscription was going to be required to raise funds.

The terms of the subscription notice itself declare the importance of not only Clydesdale Cricket Club, but of the game of cricket and its continuance as a social sport in Scotland.

"We the subscribers, being desirous to encourage the game of cricket in Scotland, and in particularly in the neighbourhood of a commercial city like Glasgow, as not only an amusement to young men engaged at business life of the day, but as a vigorous healthy and manly pursuit and being same, that through the efforts of some of the cricketers of Glasgow, a Club was originated a few years ago, Called the Clydesdale Cricket Club, which has attained a higher standing in the cricketing world than could have been expected in so short a time and learning that the members have obtained ground, which is well situated for this purpose, but which does require a sum of not under £2000 to put it into proper condition for the game: We in earnest to assist them, hereby subscribe the sum marked opposite our respective signatures; but under the express condition that the money so subscribed, be applied to no other purpose than for the putting and maintaining the ground, in good and proper condition for the Game of Cricket."

The major architects of "Big House" cricket contributed to the subscription, along with other cricket clubs and members of the public. Such names as the Earl of Eglinton and Winton, Sir John Maxwell, the Earls of Glasgow, Douglas and Dalkeith, the Duke of Hamilton, Sir Michael Shaw Stewart, Sir Archibald Campbell of Blythswood, Sir Archibald Campbell of Garscube, Carrick Buchanan of Drumpellier, James Ewing and John Tennant, local Members of Parliament such as Robert Dalglish, Alexander Dunn and Henry Bruce and cricket clubs such as Greenock are all listed.

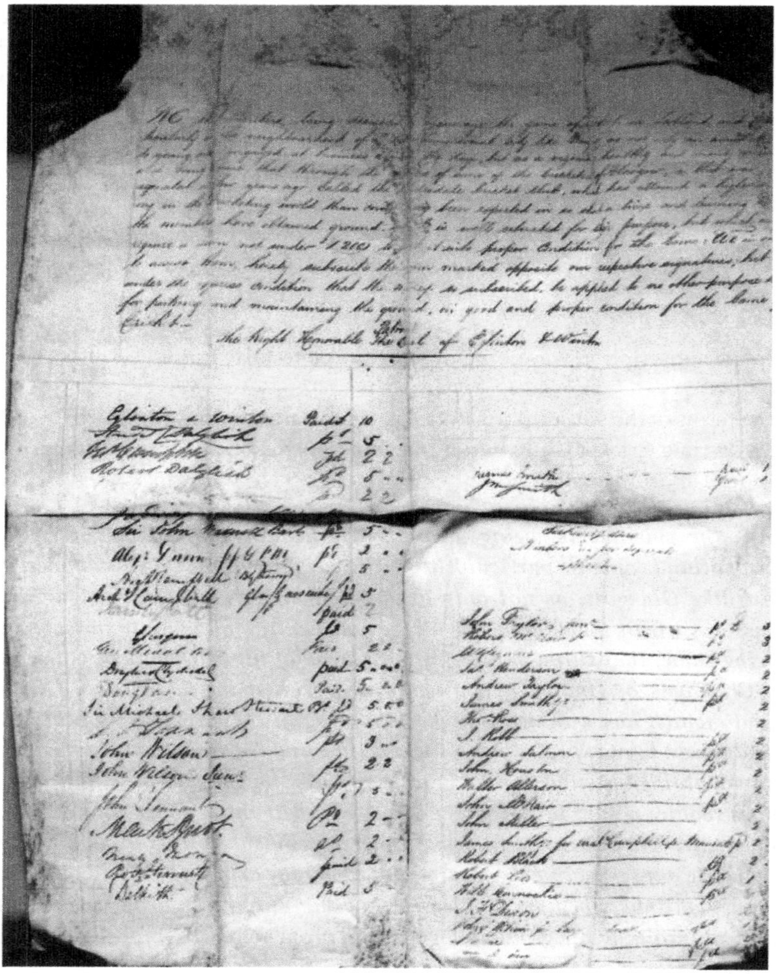

It may just be coincidental that the railway construction was being carried out by the Caledonian Railway Company of whom William Dixon was the major shareholder, but Clydesdale's future would be finally secured by its move to land leased from the Pollok Estate under a beneficial feu agreement and that it would be eventually surrounded by railways, streets and houses.

However, the construction of the Cathcart Railway compelled the Town Council to give notice to quit to many institutions, business and clubs, as the ground that they occupied by ownership or lease would be required for the building the new railway.

Queen's Park Football Club would be one such institution/club that would be affected by such change, and in doing so, the ripple effect of this change lapped at the shores on other clubs, and their future destinies.

By April 1882, Queen's Park secured land north of their then Hampden site (Cathkin) for the construction of a new ground with the intent for it to be ready for the commencement of the 1884-1885 season, but until the precise routes of the railway construction were finally determined, the club would have to seek alternative facilities to continue playing.

After discussion with Third Lanark Rifle Volunteers and Clydesdale, arrangements were made for Queen's Park Football Club to train on Tuesdays and Thursdays at Third Lanark's ground and in July 1883, agreement was made with the Clydesdale Cricket Club for use of Titwood Park and the pavilion for the forthcoming football season, at a rental of £60.00.

But changes would have to be made to Clydesdale's ground, Titwood, to facilitate the temporary relocation of Queen's Park Football Club.

As one can see from the 1893 Ordnance Survey map of Titwood, the ground was very differently sized, shaped and structured from what it is today, however, its proximity to Crossmyloof Railway Station remains.

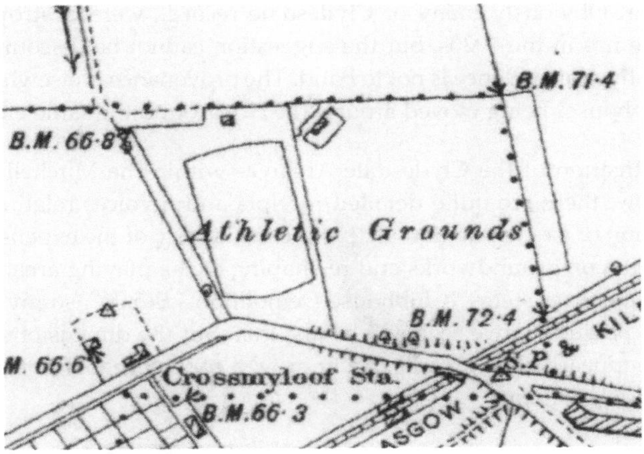

Interestingly, with the expansion of the Cathcart Railway, two further stations were created close to Clydesdale in Maxwell Park and Pollokshields West along with the many roads and streets that presently surround the ground.

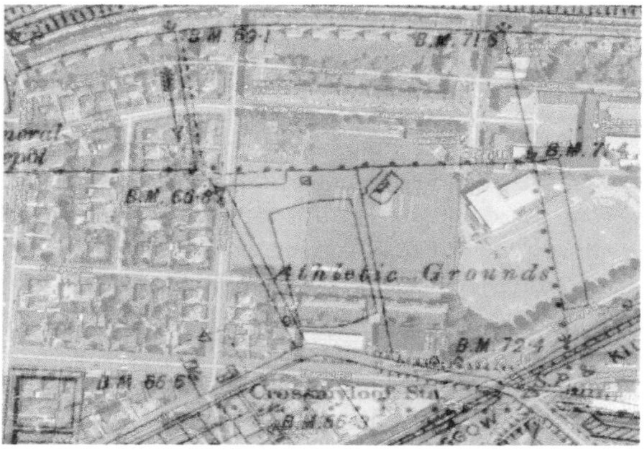

However, the main pavilion is differently located to the present one. In the map, it is top-centre whereas now, the pavilion is located top right.

The shape and structure of the clubhouse, as per all the various Ordnance Survey maps of 1894, fits exactly on top of the current clubhouse if superimposed, and given that the Pollokshields Athletics Club pavilion was put on rollers and pushed across Pollok Estate to become Poloc Cricket Club's pavilion, it is entirely plausible that something similar was done at Titwood and the relocation of the clubhouse from one part of the ground to another. Obviously many of Clydesdale records were destroyed in a clubhouse fire in the 1920s, but the suggestion cannot be discounted just because physical evidence is not to hand. The provenance is elsewhere with other clubhouses being moved around the city around the same era.

On investigation of the Clydesdale Archives within the Mitchell Library in Glasgow, there are quite detailed receipts and invoices relating to the construction of a new pavilion for 1904. The majority of the expense seems to have been on groundworks and re-shaping of the playing area, but one of the final entries states "Clubhouse Demolition - £15.00", so my fanciful hope of a pavilion move seems to be just that. But the dimensions of both pavilions appear to be the same. An improved copy perhaps? The frontage certainly looks similar.

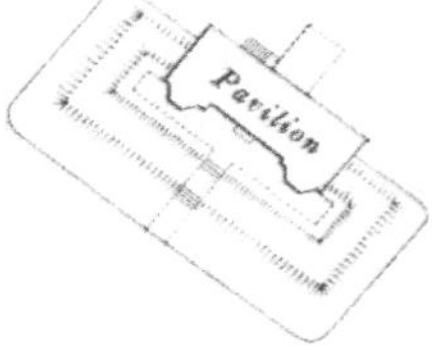

Clydesdale – Western Union Champions 1895

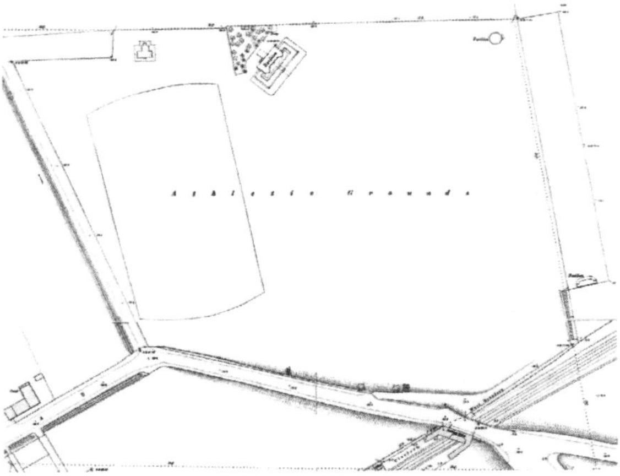

When you look at the map, on the left hand side you also see the huge playing area set aside for football and other sports.

As Clydesdale was re-developed over the next 50 years, the ground and its features changed. Part of the area that was the football ground was leased to J & P Coats by the Stirling Maxwell estate who turned the area into the company's tennis and bowls facility. It was still there in the 1980s but has been removed and replaced with further development at Clydesdale by the club, such as its astro-turf hockey pitch, as the priorities of THE premier cricket club in the Glasgow area alter once more in an ever-changing culture of accessible and relevant sporting interests tailored to meet the demands of the members of this club.

The 'Spiders' Spell of Spin at Titwood

With Queen's Park Football Club using Clydesdale Cricket Club's ground of Titwood for the 1883-84 football season, it allowed the "Spiders" to concentrate on its new ground being built that would be named Hampden. The former ground would still exist and would later become the home of Third Lanark and re-named Cathkin. Third Lanark's ground at Southern Cricket Club's ground in Inglefield Street would remain for some time thereafter and remain as the parade ground for the Third Lanark Rifle Volunteers and later as a secondary parade ground and barracks for the Cameronian Scottish Rifles who had a parade ground in nearby Kingarth Street and Company headquarters in Coplaw Street.

Some important games were played by Queen's Park during its short tenureship at Titwood in 1883-84. The first was against Northern on Saturday 27th October 1883 which Queen's won 3-1, Their next home fixture was against Dumbarton whom they also beat 3-1. On Saturday 1st December 1883, Queen's Park played Manchester in an English Football Association Cup tie and proceeded to beat their English opposition 15-0. On Saturday 22nd December 1883, Cartvale were the opposition in a Scottish Cup tie who were soundly beaten 6-1. 1884 was brought in at Titwood with Queen's Park playing an exhibition match against London Swifts who were on the receiving end of a 5-1 thrashing. Four days later on 5th January, Pollokshields were beaten 2-1.

But probably the most important game of the 1883-84 season, and the justification for Queen's Park seeking the use of their good friends Clydesdale's ground, was when Queen's Park drew Aston Villa in the next round of the English Football Association Cup. The date was Saturday 19th January 1884, and with the proximity of Crossmyloof Station, Aston Villa brought a travelling support of more than a thousand people who travelled in a commissioned train for this fixture. You could argue that this was probably one of the earliest examples of a "football special".

Aston Villa were slaughtered 6-1 by Queen's Park, and according to the press reports of the day, *"Such was the dismay and disgust at the performance of their team, the travelling support sought other means of consolation, and drowned their sorrows to such an extent, many failed to return on time for the departure of the train for the South, and slept off their grief in unexpected, and exposed, havens of rest."*

Queen's Park completed their remaining fixtures at Titwood in time for the commencement of the 1884 cricket season. The new Hampden opened on Saturday 18th October 1884 with Dumbarton, another cricket cum football club providing the opposition, and drawing an opening attendance of over seven thousand people to admire the new ground and witness a 0-0 draw.

The Teaching of the 'Professors'

The fixture at Titwood on Saturday 19th January 1884 is of far greater significance than has been previously considered. If one puts aside the game and the result, and look at various aspects of the match itself, you are left with certain facts that have been overlooked and unappreciated.

Queen's Park are the exponents of a style of football that is radical, innovative and sophisticated and is much admired by all that watch or play against them. The employment of fitness and training regimes, combined with the tactics, set pieces and elaborate passages of play that they introduce to the game are the building blocks of what we now classify as modern football.

Many Scots are moving down south to England and taking with them a style of play called the "passing game" that English clubs start to adopt. These émigrés are referred to as the "Scotch Professors" and Queen's Park are playing a Fourth Round tie in the Football Association Challenge Cup against an Aston Villa side taught by lecturers fully conversant in the didactics of their own doctrine.

One such man was Archie Hunter. Born in 1859 in Joppa, Ayrshire, he was a talented centre-forward who had played for Third Lanark. In 1878 he moved to Birmingham and joined Aston Villa.

There were fellow Scots at Aston Villa at the time. George Ramsay was the captain, and William McGregor, although an average footballer, was a man who possessed great administration skills. The three became great friends and Hunter, Ramsay and McGregor, keen to establish a reputation for the club, introduced the concept of the "passing game" that was used in Scotland compared to England, where most club sides played a style called the "dribbling game".

Graham McColl, the author of a superb book, Aston Villa: 1874-1998: states within *"It was a style of play modelled on that which was prevalent in Scotland at the time and which had been pioneered by Queen's Park, the Glasgow side. This type of sophisticated teamwork had rarely been employed in England. Instead, individuals would try to take the ball as far as they could on their own until stopped by an opponent."*

George Ramsay retired from playing in 1882 with Hunter replacing him as captain of the club. Ramsay became the club secretary and Aston Villa, under the guidance of Hunter, Ramsay and McGregor, reached the quarter-finals of the FA Cup in 1883 and 1884.

Obviously Caledonian pride, the weather, the travel journey and the expectations of a mainly partisan crowd of 10,000 are all factors attributable to the result and Queen's Park winning the tie so convincingly, but there is an admiration of the boldness of Aston Villa Football Club in that they are prepared to adopt a concept of play and then use it against its original architects on their home turf in a competitive match.

Later on in 1884, Queen's Park travelled down to Birmingham to play a friendly game against Aston Villa. Archie Hunter later recalled *"no sooner had we begun to take up our positions for the match than pigeons could be seen flying from all parts bearing away the news that the battle had begun."* Aston Villa won the match 2-1 with Hunter commenting *"I was followed home by a multitude roaring as if I had won the Battle of Waterloo"*.

On 4th January 1890, Archie Hunter suffered a heart attack during a match against Everton. On medical advice, he subsequently retired from football having scored 42 goals in 73 first-class games, 33 of which were in the principal competition of the day, the FA Cup.

Later on in 1890, Hunter wrote a series of articles for the Birmingham Weekly Mercury recounting his times playing for Aston Villa. These same articles were collated and then published as a book, Triumphs of the Football Field.

Archie Hunter, *Triumphs of the Football Field* (1890)

I am convinced that it (football) will maintain its position as the most popular game in this country and that it will remain at the head of scientific sports. There is one enthusiasm for cricket and another for football and the enthusiasm for the latter game appears to me to be excited by deeper and heartier feelings.

At all events I have no fear that football will decline, though I am sorry that it is so largely maintained by the professional element. Speaking as a professional myself, I may say that I can only look upon professionalism as an unavoidable misfortune. While it is of immense assistance to the game in many respects, it appears to me that it lowers its character and I myself should have felt happier very often if I could have continued to play as an amateur and so regarded the game as a game and not as a business. However, this is a matter for the Association to deal with.

I should like, as one who has been credited with some success in dealing with a football team, to offer a little advice to captains - to those who are not accustomed to their duties yet, or who may be called upon at some future time to assume the position. First and foremost I would impress this upon them - treat the players as men and not as schoolboys. I have seen a great deal of mischief resulting from neglect to do this. When the players are only treated as boys they are apt to regard themselves as boys and act accordingly. They become selfish, obstinate and quarrelsome, turn sulky if they are displeased, or wrangle with one another on the field. Insubordination can never be provided against unless every player is made to feel that he will be called to account as a man and I am certain that this system works well.

Then let all prejudices be avoided. I have known Scotchmen or Welshmen disliked by Englishmen simply on account of their nationality and I have known Scotchmen and Welshmen act just in the same way towards Englishmen. Now these prejudices ought to be stamped out. The team, however it is composed, must play as a team and not as a gathering of different men out of harmony with each other. I always tried to foster good feeling in Aston Villa and I think we were one of the merriest and happiest teams in the country. For myself I never bothered my head about the country a man came from and as long as we had good players and good fellows among us, it mattered not whether they were English, Scotch or Welsh.

Archie Hunter comes across as a fascinating character who regards himself as a custodian of the ethics of fairness and playing the game for the sake of playing. Yes, he is one of the earliest recorded professional footballers and he admits openly that he would have preferred to have remained playing under the original amateur ideals, but his advice to football captains is unquestionably rooted from cricket – the preamble to the laws, the spirit of the game and the Captain's responsibility. His advice still resonates over 120 years later.

Archie Hunter died of heart failure in a Birmingham hospital on 29th November 1894. He was only 35 years old.

Within the pages of an excellently informative book, The Essential Aston Villa, the authors Adam Ward and Jeremy Griffin point out: *"Archie Hunter was a Victorian sporting celebrity. He was Aston Villa's first truly great footballer and was the idol of the Perry Barr supporters for more than a decade. Archie was a forward who played the game with a rare blend of power and skill, and his strength was a particularly useful quality at a time when barging and kicking were often considered legitimate defensive tactics."*

Archie Hunter's close friend and associate, William McGregor, would go on to become the founder of the English Football League.

Born in Braco, Perthshire, in 1846, McGregor had experienced football in its infancy in Scotland, and having moved to the Birmingham area in 1870, he opened a draper's shop, which even sold football kit, which in turn meant his place of business became an important meeting place for early football enthusiasts.

With having involvement with Aston Villa, McGregor saw the rise of professionalism within association football in England. He was the first to recognise that the new sport was in danger of splintering itself with the threats of breakaway leagues and structures, and in doing so, he suggested that there should be a league competition that created an organised calendar of fixtures for its member clubs. McGregor had been an early protagonist in trying to get baseball established in England and many have claimed that he was simply trying to copy the template that had been used to develop league baseball in North America. But McGregor himself always stated that the English County Cricket Championship was the model he preferred.

Such was his determination to establish a competitive league structure, he wrote to a number of clubs and invited them to a meeting to discuss the topic.

The content of the letter was as follows:

Every year it is becoming more and more difficult for football clubs of any standing to meet their friendly engagements and even arrange friendly matches. The consequence is that at the last moment, through cup-tie interference, clubs are compelled to take on teams who will not attract the public. I beg to tender the following suggestion as a means of getting over the difficulty: that ten or twelve of the most prominent clubs in England combine to arrange home-and-away fixtures each season, the said fixtures to be arranged at a friendly conference about the same time as the International Conference. This combination might be known as the Association Football Union, and could be managed by representative from each club. Of course, this is in no way to interfere with the National Association; even the suggested matches might be played under cup-tie rules. However, this is a detail. My object in writing to you at present is merely to draw your attention to the subject, and to suggest a friendly conference to discuss the matter more fully. I would take it as a favour if you would kindly think the matter over, and make whatever suggestions you deem necessary. I am only writing to the following – Blackburn Rovers, Bolton Wanderers, Preston North End, West Bromwich Albion, and Aston Villa, and would like to hear what other clubs you would suggest. I am, yours very truly, William McGregor (Aston Villa F.C.) P.S. How would Friday, 23 March 1888, suit for the friendly conference at Anderton's Hotel, London?

The Football League was hereby created and in September 1888, twelve clubs commenced play in a league competition that has now become the stuff of dreams, aspirations and legend, created by a Scot, who had used cricket's structure for inspiration.

The Turning of the Leaves

I have mentioned many clubs and some remain and continue either as cricket or football clubs, but there are many former cricket clubs who had fleeting experiences with football and its establishment as the national winter sport. There has to be an acknowledgment of the contribution of the "lost" cricket clubs that paved the way for football to become the global sport that it is today.

1832 Glasgow Albyn
1838 Barrhead
1850 Caledonian
1852 Paisley Thistle
1854 Blythswood
1858 Ayr Eglinton: Clutha
1860 Airdrie: Arthurlie: Bridge of Weir Thistle: Western
1862 Busby: Kirkintilloch
1863 Carluke Thistle
1866 Kilbirnie: Alexandra
1867 Glasgow Derby
1868 Dumbreck: Lenzie: East Stirlingshire
1869 Glasgow Arden: Ardrossan Castle: Bothwell
1870 Southern; Pollokshields
1872 Glasgow Lorne
1873 Glasgow Bridgetoun
1874 Glasgow Cumberland: First Lanarkshire Rifle Volunteers
1876 Glasgow Camden: Ardeer: Bearsden

The numbers of operational cricket clubs in the Glasgow area, in the mid 1870s, were on a scale previously not appreciated. My rough calculations suggest upwards of 120 and there may be more that still have to be unearthed.

There were the big clubs who I have listed. There were the many that gave football a try but there were still a lot more playing cricket and cricket alone who have been forgotten.

Rosslyn	Clifton
Walmer	Hampton
Alma	Athole
Grosvenor	Clutha
Neptune	Grovepark
Carlton	Garnetbank
Albert	Avondale
Landsdowne	Oaklands
Eglinton	Mountaineer
Standard	South Western
Argyle	Royal Oak
Albany	Winton
Grange	Holyrood
Lothian	Waverly
St.Clair	Devon
Royal Albert	Meadowside
Clyde	Adelphi
Sackville	Dowanside
Balmoral	Morning Star
Artizan	Bellgrove

With the Scottish Cup in full swing by 1876, it was evident that the new sport of football was sweeping across Scotland on a wave of enthusiasm. New teams were appearing and entering the cup that had been formed as football clubs first and foremost, but the cricket clubs were still the major participants and continued to enter their teams.

In the First Round of the 1876/1877 Scottish Cup, the following cricket clubs had entered:

Glasgow Western	Ayr Eglinton
1st Lanark RV	Vale of Leven
Thornliebank	Helensburgh
3rd Lanark RV	Alexandra
Glasgow Eastern	Kilbirnie
Arthurlie	Barrhead
Drumpellier	Busby
Cumnock	Clydesdale
Dumbarton	Dumbreck
Renton	Glasgow Northern
Glasgow Caledonian	Lennox
Lenzie	Kilmarnock
Airdrie	Blythswood

Indeed, from the formation of the Scottish Football Association with Queen's Park gathering the interested cricket clubs together for the inaugural meeting in the Dewar's Temperance Hotel, 11 Bridge Street, Glasgow on 13th March 1873, the cricket clubs would continue with participation in the Scottish Cup for a number of years to come, but it would all suddenly come to an abrupt halt.

The decisive moments that forever re-shaped the symbiotic relationships of mutual benefit between the cricket clubs, who had the infrastructure of facilities and players, and the football teams who used these players and the grounds, and led to the separation of their interests, all happened relatively quickly.

The cricket clubs, their patrons, the land-owners and the cricketers had all been affected by a combination of factors that triggered an exudation that compromised their structures and possible continuance. Over the course of a siege lasting twelve short years, the defences of cricket in the west of Scotland were at the point of disintegration.

The clubs could cope with unforeseen circumstances and events impacting on them by tackling them head on, one or maybe two impinging issues at any given time, but faced with a relentless onslaught of ever-changing difficulties and challenges, their existences, for most of them, had become terminally untenable.

The grounds on which they played were being built upon, their clubhouses were being disassembled, their patrons and land-owners were now concentrating on their business and financial interests, their members were becoming increasingly focused on their livelihoods and for all concerned, every single shilling that they possessed was now a prisoner.

Association football was an appealing pastime for all classes to turn to as a form of recreation. It could be played anywhere in any climatical condition. It was not dependent on being a member of a club to have a game. It helped, but it would be easier to be a member of a team that simply turned up at wherever, hoofed the leather for 90 minutes or so and then retired to whatever other amusement took their fancy, than being a member of a club to play a sport that required planning, preparation, commitment, dedication, expenditure and of course, favourable weather.

But even association football faced its difficulties while the sport was still in its relative infancy. Having captured the imagination of the people, the lure of pecuniary gain raised its head and divided opinion.

Since the formation of the Scottish Football Association in 1873, the member clubs would play friendly matches and various Scottish Cup and local cup ties. However, with football in England turning professional in 1885 followed by the formation of the Football League in 1888, the lure of receiving a high salary to play football was particularly appealing to many

Scottish players which led to a sudden exodus of talent south. These players were given the nickname of Scotch Professors and enjoyed the monies on offer.

By the beginning of 1890, a number of Scottish clubs were considering forming their own league to participate in. Renton took the lead and invited thirteen other clubs to discuss this subject, which they accepted apart from Queen's Park and Clyde.

Queen's Park, the founding father of Scottish football and one of the major driving forces behind the development of the game, were utterly opposed to the creation of a league structure citing that it would lead to professionalism and would also be detrimental to the interests of the smaller clubs. Queen's Park's principled stance of playing the game for the sake of playing and protecting the sport as an amateur recreation proved to be correct as six of the founder members would leave this new league structure by 1900.

Queen's Park was somewhat prescient in stating that professionalism would be detrimental to the interests of the smaller clubs. The Scottish Cup campaigns of 1889/90 and 1890/91 had around twenty five cricket clubs participating, but there were none in the 1891/92 competition. The professional Scottish Football League had arrived and the number of non-league clubs in the cup was reduced.

There were still "cricket" clubs participating but only in reference to origin as they were essentially devolved sections from the parent cricket club and would become separate entities as professional football clubs. Twenty of the current senior Scottish football association clubs in 2012 were originally associated with cricket clubs.

Of course Queen's Park and teams like Clyde would eventually end up participating in a professionalised Scottish football league structure, but Queen's Park have always remained adherents of the amateur status and have done so for nearly 150 years.

The heady days of association football dominated by cricketers and their clubs were at an end as professionalisation at senior and junior level had arrived.

The multi-faceted reasons behind the cull of the Glasgow area cricket clubs triggered a reaction from its survivors. They enjoyed protection from extinction because they either owned or had long term leases of their grounds and had not been ear-marked for development.

The larger of these cricket clubs in the west, comprising of Clydesdale, Drumpellier, Greenock, Poloc, Uddingston and West of Scotland came together to form the Western Union cricket league in 1893, leaving the smaller clubs to consolidate themselves under the panels of its umbrella, eking out their respective existences with the playing of friendlies as they had done so previously.

The new Western Union cricket league retained the amateur status for its players, but the clubs were allowed to have a professional cricketer, and most did employ one for playing and coaching purposes but also for ground preparation duties.

But the issue of professionalism is a thorny one and has been the case in west cricket for 150 years. The Glasgow Select versus Edinburgh Select matches had been played for over 20 years but were abandoned in 1894 as disputes over the introduction of professionalism finally killed off the fixture. In 1910, the Western Union Championship was contested without Clydesdale, Drumpellier, Greenock and West of Scotland, who temporarily withdrew from the league claiming that the majority of the clubs that they played against relied far too heavily on the performances of their professionals.

The argument still rages in the 21st Century and whether a match professional is actually a necessary requirement or should the clubs concentrate on having professionalised coaches to develop the skills of their members and engage the community by providing opportunities for all to experience cricket. The traditional values of the cricket in the west, where the clubs involved the communities for the communities to engage the clubs, would suggest following the latter option while maintaining the original ethics, but then again, the evils of short term solutions and the chasing of silverware have always befallen the clubs, but it is not a sustainable, or even healthy, undertaking for the clubs to now pursue.

The Western Union cricket league became the first competitive league structure for cricket in Scotland, and remained as a competitive league for over a century. It had its many detractors and critics, who sneered at these Glasgow area clubs and its "closed shop" league structure and accused them of elitism, parochialism, insularity along with suggestions that the general ethos of the league was detrimental to the furtherance of the game, not only in the west of Scotland, but the rest of the country.

But this same Western Union cricket league, and what eventually turned out to be its traditional composition of ten clubs, had been a league that had been borne in the face of almost terminal adversity. These ten clubs were the surviving children created by the marriages of "Big House" cricket, and of course they would be protectionist of their kith and kin. These ten clubs were committed to preserve the integrity of its cricket and to maintain, at the very least, the egalitarian and altruistic principles that had led to their original creation and the type of cricket that they played.

This was a league that had dealt with the numerous difficulties it faced every generation. The impact of the Great War, the Great Depression of the 1930s, the Second World War, post war austerity right through to the social and economic changes of the 1970s. From 1980 onwards, the clubs had to adapt to the new changes that were appearing in society, and that there was now freedom of choice.

It had survived for over a century, but like all things, it had had to adapt itself to evolve to allow further generations to enjoy its legacy.

When the old Western Union and the Glasgow & District Leagues merged to create the Western District Cricket Union in 1996, subconsciously, all of the clubs concerned had looked at their pasts to find the answer to their future in a new century and its respective challenges.

The Western District Cricket Union's mission statement for the 21st Century is proof enough of that claim:

"We are a Union of Clubs, a collective of equals willing and determined to assist any club, to help them develop, improve and survive even in difficult times and we do everything in our power to stabilise and ensure the viability of all our member clubs, no matter how big or small."

That is not a declaration of intent, it is more than that. It is a statement of fact.

Cricket's Impact on the Football Codes

The cricket club structure from the mid 1850s onwards created unexpected opportunities for communities to mix. A welcome by-product created by the "Big House" cricket equation perhaps?

venue + resources + players = game + networks + opportunity

The clubs became focal points for local populations to frequent, free from the toils of labour and providing access to recreation whilst conforming to the expectations of Victorian society.

In the midst of industrialisation, colonialisation and expansion, an explosion of enthusiasm for sport had occurred. Rowing and cricket were the recreational super-powers of the day, and cricket had inadvertently provided the opportunity for the experimentation of alternate sports for the winter months.

Across the British Isles, rugby and football took off. Depending on the geography and the demographics, the preference for which of the football codes resulted. In the north of England, rugby league became gospel, rugby union was encamped in Wales and the south of England and in the west of Scotland, association football triggered amongst the population an unprecedented propinquity for the sport.

In Ireland, and it has to be appreciated here that while Glasgow was the Second City of the Empire, Dublin was classified as the Third; the impact of organised team sport was substantial.

Cricket in Ireland has a longer history than Scotland, and has been played there for nearly 300 years with references being made to the earliest game in 1730. Its strongholds are in and around the cities of Dublin, Londonderry and Belfast, with records showing clubs springing up therein from the 1830s onwards. The earliest recorded match however was in 1792 when an "All Ireland" select played the British Garrison in Dublin.

This "All Ireland" select featured players such as an Arthur Wellesley, who later became the Duke of Wellington, and a Major Hobart and a Mr. Thomas Brisbane, both of whom went on to give their names to Australian state capitals. It is interesting to note that Thomas Brisbane was born near Greenock, and after his death, the street that which Greenock Cricket Club now stands, was named in his memory. He was laid to rest not far from where he grew up.

But Ireland had its own football sport called "caid" or what we now recognise as Gaelic football.

During the 1860s and 1870s, rugby started to become popular in Ireland and when the rules of association football were codified and issued in 1863, Gaelic football was in danger of being replaced by a "rough-and-tumble game" that the cricketers of the land turned to in the winter months. Association football had taken hold in the emerald isle and had consumed the whole of Ulster by the 1880s.

Such was the concern of traditionalists to protect its heritage sports, the Gaelic Athletic Association was formed in 1884 and when conjoined with Irish society becoming politically divided, cricket, football and rugby's association with mainland Britain, the aristocracy and privilege, cost it many adherents. The Gaelic Athletic Association even took the bold measures of placing a ban on foreign sports being played, but cricket, football and rugby prevailed against adversity. The Irish Football League is the second oldest in the world after England with Scotland being third.

In Australia, football is not a major sport, with cricket, Australian Rules Football, rugby union and rugby league being ahead of association football in the pecking order.

Nowadays, with an increasing population descended from immigrants outside of the sphere of what was once British colonialism, football, or soccer, is becoming extremely popular and attractive for young Australians to play. However, football, of a sort, was played in the Melbourne area in the 1850s with the earliest recorded match being played on 15th June 1858 between Scotch College and Melbourne Grammar School.

In the Australian National Archives and the Melbourne Cricket Club database, I found the following letter by a certain Tom Wills that was published in the 'Bell's Life in Victoria & Sporting Chronicle' on the 10th July 1858, calling for a "foot-ball club", or some other "athletic game", with a "code of laws" to keep cricketers fit during winter to be developed and introduced.

The letter has become the single most important document in the creation of a new code of football in 1859, that new code being Australian Rules Football and deservedly, this letter is now regarded as a national treasure by Australia.

Winter Practice

To the Editor of "Bell's Life in Victoria and Sporting Chronicle" Saturday July 10, 1858

SIR, - Now that cricket has been put aside for some few months to come, and cricketers have assumed somewhat of the chrysalis nature (for a time only 'tis true), but at length will again burst forth in all their varied hues, rather than allow this state of torpor to creep over them, and stifle their new supple limbs, why can they not, I say, form a foot-ball club, and form a committee of three or four to draw up a code of laws?

If a club of this sort were got up, it would be of a vast benefit to any cricket-ground to be trampled upon, and would make the turf quite firm and durable; besides which it would keep those who are inclined to become stout from having their joints encased in useless superabundant flesh.

If it is not possible to form a foot-ball club, why should not these young men who have adopted this new-born country for their motherland, why I say, do they not form themselves into a rifle club, so as at any rate they may be some day called to aid their adopted land against a tyrant's band, that may some day "pop" upon us when we least expect a foe at our very doors. Surely our young cricketers are not afraid of the crack of the rifle, when they face so courageously the leathern sphere and it would disgrace no one to learn in time how to defend his country and his hearth. A firm heart, a steady hand, and a quick eye, are all that are requisite, and, with practice, all these may be attained.

Trusting that someone will take up the matter, and form either of the above clubs, or, at any rate, some athletic games, I remain, yours truly,

T.W. Wills

A few weeks after the publication of the letter by Tom Wills in the 'Bell's Life in Victoria & Sporting Chronicle', the paper then published on 31st July 1858, a notice it had received from a James Bryant who was a professional cricketer for the Melbourne Cricket Club and was the proprietor of The Parade Hotel beside the Melbourne Cricket Ground.

James Bryant offered to provide a foot-ball for anyone that wanted to play a game at one o'clock that day in Richmond Park. The subsequent newspaper reports of this match were as follows:

"Around forty men including some 'pedestrian athletes' turned up to form a 'St Kilda Scratch Team' and a 'Melbourne Scratch Team'. Trees were used for goal

posts. There were no boundaries and the game lasted from 1pm till dark and the greatest good humor prevailed until the ball could no longer be seen. Englanders' played something resembling Rugby', Scotlanders, 'a game that defied description', Irelanders 'yelled and punted the ball in the air' while others 'played with no rules at all'."

"On 31 July, a knock-a-bout match at Yarra Park was played between a "St Kilda scratch team" and "Melbourne scratch team". Trees were used for goal posts and there were no boundaries and the match lasted from 1 p.m. until dark. There were no rules and fights frequently broke out. "

And depending on which report one reads, this game on 31st July 1858 was abandoned as confusion over the rules caused fights to break out amongst the participants. Or by simply using a superb euphemism *"the greatest good humor prevailed until the ball could no longer be seen."*

The seed had been sown and an embryonic version of Australian Rules Football was born. Within a year, it had been developed, codified, and the un-used cricket grounds in winter became the perfect places to play this new sport while enabling the cricketers to keep fit during the off-season.

And this still remains the case 150 years later.

As an addendum to the above, my personal favourite passage in one of the press reports is the following:

"Englanders' played something resembling Rugby', Scotlanders, 'a game that defied description', Irelanders 'yelled and punted the ball in the air' while others 'played with no rules at all',"

Maybe the reporter was being somewhat prophetic and telling us all something 150 odd years in advance?

As The Willow Vanishes

Every time that I am in the clubhouse at Clydesdale Cricket Club, I always feel that there is a presence very close by, just out of my sight and whispering to me, trying to tell me something that I cannot hear. It is a very hard sensation to describe and I suppose the closest description would be like you trying to visualise the ghost of a smile that has faded away. You can remember seeing it but you cannot picture it.

This strange sensation never fails to occur, and when I am in the pavilion at Clydesdale, I always end up looking at all the photographs on the clubhouse walls and staring at the faces of familiar friends who cannot recall my name.

However, there is a single photograph whose personal poignancy for me triggers the memories of all of my childhood, youth and adulthood with flash-backs of incidents and the familiarities of friendships lost, forgotten, broken and found.

The photograph in question is of an invitational cricket match played at Clydesdale on Sunday 9th July 1967. It portrays two cricket teams and officials in front of the crowded steps of the clubhouse. Among the cricketers are some of the greatest players in the world at the time. I always look at this photograph as it is the only one in existence that features all of my birth family together at the same time.

After nearly 50 years of exposure to sunlight, the vibrancy of its colours are beginning to fade and the clarity is starting to dissipate, but this photograph itself is a snapshot of a significant moment in Scottish sporting history in many ways.

I have always looked at it from a personal view in that it captures the most important point in my family history with us all being pictured together at a single moment in time. Within a few months of this photograph being taken, my sister Elizabeth, bright eyed and full of the hopes and dreams of a whole life to look forward to, discovers that she has a terminal form of cancer, and with her passing early in 1970, the brightness within a family unit dimmed forever.

I have the same mental routine every time I study this picture - I always have the hope that maybe the following has happened since I last looked:

I check to see if the ash has fallen from the cigarette in my father's hand as he sits in the front row as President of Clydesdale Cricket Club. No.

I look along the front row at my brother Douglas, the match scorer for the day, to see if he started smiling. He hasn't.

Another brother, Eric, is careering down the clubhouse steps in pursuit of a two bob bit he has just dropped. He hasn't caught it.

William, my eldest brother, tries to chat up a pretty brunette in the crowd. Still trying but with no success.

My sister Elizabeth still hasn't finished the conversation with her friend Janet.

And finally I find my mother, who with the dignified skill that only comes from being a mother of five, is still continuing a conversation while adjusting her hat and wiping the snot from my face at the same time.

But the other important aspect of this photograph, and it was only when I starting collating all the evidence together to begin writing this book that I suddenly realised its true significance - this is a pictorial record of the final ever fixture of "Big House" cricket to be played in Scotland.

A hundred odd years of Glasgow's forgotten collective socio, economic, political and sporting heritage are colliding together, for a final time, in an event to be left for posterity for future generations to reflect upon.

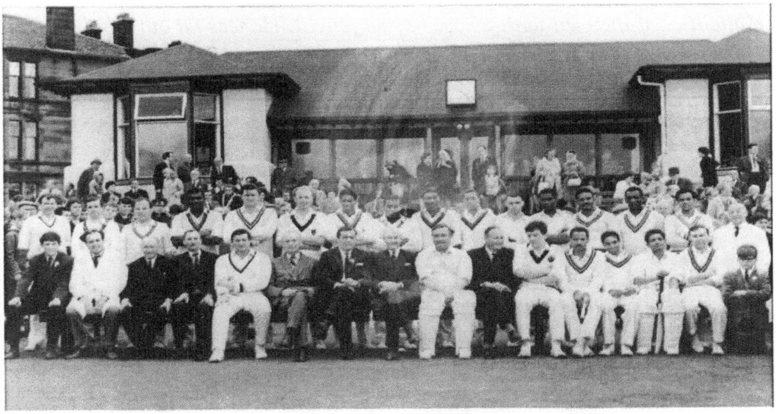

This is a full circle rotation whereby, gathered together for a single day at Clydesdale Cricket Club, along with some of the greatest cricketers in the world of the time, are the last men standing that are representative of the concept of "Big House" cricket, and all of them are there for altruistic reasons – for an exhibition match to be played to raise funds for the Scottish Branch of the National Playing Fields Association.

But there is a hidden significance that makes this photograph such an important and declarative piece of Scotland's sporting history. The two teams themselves are in fact the assembled champions of the last two men standing who were completely representative of the ideals that "Big House" cricket had produced.

Sir Alec Douglas Home had been Prime Minister of the United Kingdom and had also played First Class cricket representing Oxford University Cricket Club, Middlesex CCC and the MCC. He was President of the MCC when this match took place. Although he was a beneficiary of various family estates, he had pursued a lifelong career in politics because of the widespread unemployment and poverty to be found in the Scottish lowlands and he wished to help those communities.

Lord Clydesmuir was in fact Ronald John Bilsland Colville, director of Colvilles Limited, a company that was nationalised and became British Steel in 1967. He had been a soldier with the Cameronians (Scottish Rifles), a regiment famously recruited from Glasgow and the Lanarkshire area, the industrial heart of Scotland and saw action at Dunkirk, Italy and the D-Day Normandy landings. He had notably served as the Governor of the Bank of Scotland and was also the Lord Lieutenant of Lanarkshire and the Captain General of the Queen's Bodyguard in Scotland. His obituary in 1996 noted *"he always remained a West of Scotland man respecting and sharing the down-to-earth qualities of the men with whom he had fought. He was an outstanding and dedicated servant of Scotland."*

Denis Compton tosses the coin in the presence of Lord Clydesmuir, Sir Alec Douglas-Home and Keith Miller.

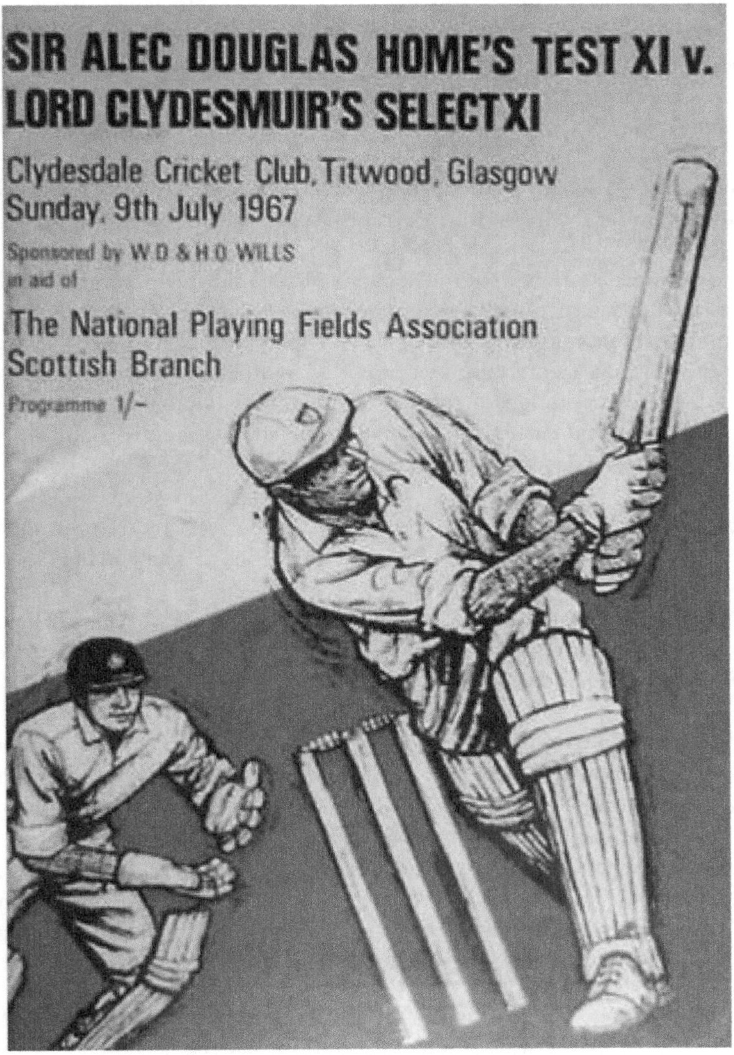

SIR ALEC DOUGLAS HOME'S TEST XI v.
LORD CLYDESMUIR'S SELECT XI
Clydesdale Cricket Club, Titwood, Glasgow
Sunday, 9th July 1967
Sponsored by W.D. & H.O. WILLS
in aid of
The National Playing Fields Association
Scottish Branch
Programme 1/-

Sir Alec Douglas Home's team was captained by the famous England cricketer Denis Compton who had also played professional football for Arsenal Football Club.

Lord Clydesmuir's select side was captained by Keith Miller, regarded as Australia's greatest ever all-rounder and accomplished Australian Rules footballer for St. Kilda. A man whom the press described that he *"was more than a cricketer ... he embodied the idea that there was more to life than simply playing cricket"*.

The venue: Titwood, the home of Clydesdale Cricket Club – a ground that was still under the feu of the local land-owner, the Pollok Estate.

The resources: Titwood for the hosting of the game, the proximity of public transport infrastructure, the neighbouring facilities such as Crossmyloof Ice Rink and Hutcheson's Grammar School for parking, the J&P Coats area for the marquees, entertainment provided by the Royal Highland Fusiliers Band, the co-operation of the City of Glasgow Police for public safety, traffic control and parking arrangements, the many volunteers and helpers, the Red Cross (Glasgow Branch) etc.

The players: Visiting overseas professionals, the West Indies touring side, Scottish internationalists, English county professionals and local players.

The game: An invitational select exhibition limited-over cup match, a novel concept for the time, featuring some of the biggest names of the day, and to be played on a Sunday which was unusual in Scotland.

The networks: To have the President of the MCC in Sir Alec Douglas Home, along with Lord Clydesmuir, Lord Forbes (Chairman of the National Playing Fields Association), Keith Miller and Dennis Compton, the majority of the West Indian touring test side, assorted overseas and homegrown professionals and local players in attendance, the use of the ground and neighbouring facilities, match sponsorship by W.D & H.O. Wills, match programme and advertising, catering and the other match requirements in place, they all had been procured by the use of the many networks cricket had created over time.

The opportunity: A cricket match to raise funds for the Scottish Branch of the National Playing Fields Association.

Sir Alec Douglas-Home's Test XI

1. D.C.S Compton, Captain (Middlesex and England)
2. K.V. Andrew (Northants and England)
3. D. Carter (West Indies)
4. C. Depeiza (West Indies)
5. L. Gibbs (Warwickshire and West Indies)
6. G. Goonesena (Nottinghamshire and Ceylon)
7. C. Griffiths (West Indies)
8. F. King (West Indies)
9. Nasim-Ul-Ghani (Pakistan)
10. C. Watson (West Indies)
11. C. Wright (West Indies)

Lord Clydesmuir's Select XI

1. K. Miller, Captain (Australia)
2. J. Brown (Perthshire and Scotland)
3. I. Davidson (Nottinghamshire)
4. W.D.F Dow (Essex and Scotland)
5. L.C. Dudman (Perthshire and Scotland)
6. R. Ellis (Kilmarnock and Scotland)
7. K.Hardie (Stenhousemuir and Scotland)
8. A. Holder (Ferguslie and Barbados)
9. T.B.Racionzer (Sussex and Scotland)
10. G.Rock (Barbados)
11. M. Siddique (Clydesdale)

Lord Clydesmuir's Select XI
205 for 9 wickets

Sir Alec Douglas-Home's Test XI
207 for 7 wickets

The year is 1967, where the winners of cricket in the west of Scotland were:

West of Scotland Cricket Club – winners of the Rothman's Quaich, the national cup competition.

Ferguslie Cricket Club – winners of the Western Union and the West League Cup.

Uddingston Cricket Club – winners of the Rowan Charity Cup.

Irvine Cricket Club – winners of the Western Cup. A club that was formed and played in the new town created in the remnants of the Eglinton Estate. A club located within a community that would benefit from this match with the design, creation and construction of a new multi-sports ground at Marress, with the assistance of Len Issott, the groundsman at West of Scotland Cricket Club.

It is the year that Celtic won an unprecedented quintuple by not only becoming the first British team to win the European Cup, but also winning the Scottish League Championship, the Scottish Cup, the Scottish League Cup, and the Glasgow Cup and with a team of players all drawn from the communities originally created and developed by the industrial explosion that led to "Big House" cricket.

1967, the same year as Scotland's football triumph over England at Wembley to become the "Champions of the World".

Sunday 9th July 1967, the exact centennial date of the founding of the Queen's Park Football Club whose motto *Ludere Causa Ludendi - "to play for the sake of playing"* exemplifies what should be the priority mission statement for all sports to follow.

The intertwining of all the random strands of the spider's web finally come together to weave the tapestry that depicts the story of a legacy. The playing of this particular game, on this specific date, was in fact a farewell salute to all the gallant pioneers of the previous decades who developed cricket to create the formation of clubs who then helped to establish football with the first ever international match to the founding of the Scottish Football Association to the first Scottish Cup Final and the taking of football around the world. Glasgow's truly forgotten sporting legacy is revealed for all to appreciate its value.

A final quote from David Drummond Bone debunks the many perceptions of both sports:

"The vagaries of the game admit of no distinction of class. The crack player is, in fine, found among all classes—in the gentleman's son, in the clerk at the desk, and the lad in the workshop. There may be different ways of working out the latent ability, but sooner or later it begins to show itself. Some thought it was scarcely fair in the Duke of Wellington to say that "Waterloo was won at Eton." There is not the least possibility of doubt such a remark might be misunderstood, and many feel inclined to charge the "Iron Duke" with ignoring the services rendered by the non-commissioned officers and men of the British army, for everybody knows that none but the sons of the opulent class can ever gain admittance to Eton.

It looked, in fact, very like the credit being given to the officers for winning that great battle. Wellington, however, had his eye on the football and cricket grounds when he spoke these words, and no doubt intended to convey the idea that these games went a long way in bracing up the nerve which served so well on the battle-field. Close adhesion to the practice of any game really and sincerely creates fresh possibilities of that perfection and discipline. And why should this not be so in a game regulated by sharply-defined maxims? And as for Wellington's remarks, the most humble member of the team may show the greatest ability."

As I enter the autumn of my playing career and the games that I have left to play are like leaves falling from a tree, when one day there are lots of them and then suddenly there are no more, I finally understand what my father was trying to explain to me all through my childhood.

As the sound of willow vanishes from our gardens, streets, parks and playing fields, and the combined pressures and attractions of modern society decrease participation in outdoor pastimes, we have lost sight of the important legacy of cricket in our national history and treat it with disdain and ignorance, and this undeserved prejudice towards cricket means its days in Scotland as a summer sport are now sadly numbered.

This dismissal of the original national team sport cannot be allowed.

The answers to its future always lie in the past. I just hope that others will now look back to search for these answers and learn from them.

Acknowledgements

Grateful thanks to the following individuals, clubs, institutions, companies, organisations and web-sites and their respective databases for the inspiration and information that they have provided:

Ayr Cricket Club
Douglas Johnstone
Clydesdale Cricket Club
Drumpellier Cricket Club
Bill McPate
East Kilbride Cricket Club
Ferguslie Cricket Club
GHK Cricket Club
Glasgow Academicals Cricket Club
Ainsley Mann
Glasgow Academicals Rugby Football Club
Hugh Barrow
Glasgow University Cricket Club
Greenock Cricket Club
Helensburgh Cricket Club
Hillhead Cricket Club
Inverclyde Cricket Club
Jim Murphy
Irvine Cricket Club
Kelburne Cricket Club
Andrew Miller
Kilmarnock Cricket Club
Motherwell Cricket Club
Poloc Cricket Club
Keith Young
Prestwick Cricket Club
Tom Halpin
Renfrew Cricket Club
Sai Majeed
Uddingston Cricket Club
Vale of Leven Cricket Club
Victoria Cricket Club
Weirs Cricket Club
West of Scotland Cricket Club
John Cameron
Paul Coffey
Western District Cricket Union
Cricket Scotland
Roddy Smith
Cricket Ireland
England and Wales Cricket Board
Marylebone Cricket Club
Melbourne Cricket Club
Patricia Downs
Scottish Football Museum at Hampden
Richard McBrearty
Queen's Park Football Club
Scottish Football Association
Scottish Football League
Scottish Junior Football Association
Historical Football Kits
Scottish Rugby Union
Irish Football Association
Irish Rugby Union
Gaelic Athletic Association
Ger Siggins
English Football Association
Glasgow University
University of Strathclyde Library, Department of Archives and Special Collections
Glasgow City Council
Glasgow Digital Library
National Archives of Australia
Cambridge University
Warwick University
The Gallant Pioneers
kerrydalestreet.co.uk
Pollokshields Heritage
Dumbreck Conservation
Glasgow Building Preservation Trust
East Ayrshire Council
South Ayrshire Council
East Dunbartonshire Council
North Lanarkshire Council
South Lanarkshire Council
East Renfrewshire Council
Renfrewshire Council
Monklands Heritage
Historic Scotland
The National Trust for Scotland
Project Gutenberg
Burkes Peerage
National Census Database
Royal Historical Society
Graces Guide
Cricinfo
Cricarchives
The Cameronians (Scottish Rifles) Museum
Ministry of Defence
Imperial War Museum
National Archives of Norway
Encyclopedia Britannica
Scottish Court Service
Urban Glasgow
The Glasgow Story
The Church of Scotland
National Library of Scotland
John Player Special

Image Index

Front Cover
Composite Picture sourced from: Young Family Collection; The Royal Commission on the Ancient and Historical Monuments of Scotland; The Scottish Football Museum at Hampden; Private Collection - Reference: WO 98/8/797; Crown Copyright;

Back Cover
Young Family Collection; Cricket Scotland; Western District Cricket Union; Fifty Years Reminiscences of Scottish Cricket – David Drummond Bone, 1898;

Page(s)

1	Young Family Collection
7	Courtesy of Alexander L Strang
11-21	Glasgow University Library Special Collection Mu26-f.56, 57
29	The Castles and Mansions of Ayrshire - Alexander Hastie Millar, 1885; Scottish Post Office Directories 1773 to 1911
30-31	Scottish Post Office Directories 1773 to 1911
33	Dagny Elise Hansen 1942 - Young Family Collection
35	Fifty Years Reminiscences of Scottish Cricket – David Drummond Bone, 1898
36	The Old Country Houses of the Old Glasgow Gentry - John Guthrie Smith and John Oswald Mitchell, 1878; Drumpellier Cricket Club
37	Scottish Post Office Directories 1773 to 1911
38	Scottish Post Office Directories 1773 to 1911
39	Memoirs and portraits of one hundred Glasgow men - James Maclehose, 1886; Fifty Years Reminiscences of Scottish Cricket – David Drummond Bone, 1898
40	Young Family Collection
41	Scottish Post Office Directories 1773 to 1911
42	Fifty Years Reminiscences of Scottish Cricket – David Drummond Bone, 1898
43	Mitchell Library, Glasgow; West of Scotland Cricket Club
44	The Old Country Houses of the Old Glasgow Gentry - John Guthrie Smith and John Oswald Mitchell, 1878
45	Poloc Cricket Club
46	Scottish Post Office Directories 1773 to 1911
49	Young Family Collection
54	The Old Country Houses of the Old Glasgow Gentry - John Guthrie Smith and John Oswald Mitchell, 1878; Scottish Post Office Directories 1773 to 1911
55	The Old Country Houses of the Old Glasgow Gentry - John Guthrie Smith and John Oswald Mitchell, 1878; Scottish Post Office Directories 1773 to 1911
56	The Old Country Houses of the Old Glasgow Gentry - John Guthrie Smith and John Oswald Mitchell, 1878; Scottish Post Office Directories 1773 to 1911
57	The Old Country Houses of the Old Glasgow Gentry - John Guthrie Smith and John Oswald Mitchell, 1878; Scottish Post Office Directories 1773 to 1911
58	The Old Country Houses of the Old Glasgow Gentry - John Guthrie Smith and John Oswald Mitchell, 1878
59	Scottish Post Office Directories 1773 to 1911
60	The Castles and Mansions of Ayrshire - Alexander Hastie Millar, 1885;

	Scottish Post Office Directories 1773 to 1911
61	Wikipedia
62	Young Family Collection
64	Douglas Johnstone of Ayr Cricket Club
65	The Old Country Houses of the Old Glasgow Gentry - John Guthrie Smith and John Oswald Mitchell, 1878
66	Young Family Collection
67	The castles and mansions of Renfrewshire and Buteshire – A H Millar 1889
68	Scottish Post Office Directories 1773 to 1911; The Guardian; kerrydal estreet.co.uk
69	Scottish Post Office Directories 1773 to 1911
70	Young Family Collection; Scottish Post Office Directories 1773 to 1911
71	Young Family Collection
72	Young Family Collection
76	Scottish Post Office Directories 1773 to 1911
77	Scottish Post Office Directories 1773 to 1911
79	Glasgow City Libraries, Information and Learning
83	Scottish Post Office Directories 1773 to 1911
84	Scottish Post Office Directories 1773 to 1911
86	Memoirs/portraits of one hundred Glasgow men - James Maclehose, 1886
87	Memoirs/portraits of one hundred Glasgow men - James Maclehose, 1886
89	Memoirs/portraits of one hundred Glasgow men - James Maclehose, 1886
90	Memoirs/portraits of one hundred Glasgow men - James Maclehose, 1886
93	The History of The Queen's Park Football Club 1867-1917 by Richard Robinson, 1920
94	The History of The Queen's Park Football Club 1867-1917 by Richard Robinson, 1920
98	Scottish Football Museum at Hampden
99	Scottish Football Museum at Hampden
100	Wikipedia
102	The Royal Commission on the Ancient and Historical Monuments of Scotland
103	The History of The Queen's Park Football Club 1867-1917 by Richard Robinson, 1920
104	The History of The Queen's Park Football Club 1867-1917 by Richard Robinson, 1920
105	Scottish Post Office Directories 1773 to 1911; Memoirs/portraits of one hundred Glasgow men - James Maclehose, 1886
106	Scottish Post Office Directories 1773 to 1911
108	Young Family Collection; BBC News
112	Scottish Post Office Directories 1773 to 1911
113	Fifty Years Reminiscences of Scottish Cricket – David Drummond Bone, 1898
114	Young Family Collection
115	National Library of Scotland; As Centuries Blend - Samuel Courtney, 1954
118	Cricinfo
119	Fred Lillywhite, 1860 - Shutup !!, The English Cricketers' Trip to Canada and the United States
121	Young Family Collection
122	Young Family Collection
124	Young Family Collection
125	The Old Country Houses of the Old Glasgow Gentry - John Guthrie

Smith and John Oswald Mitchell, 1878; Scottish Post Office Directories 1773 to 1911

126 Scottish Post Office Directories 1773 to 1911

128 Young Family Collection

129 Scottish Post Office Directories 1773 to 1911

130 Young Family Collection

131 Young Family Collection

132 The Old Country Houses of the Old Glasgow Gentry - John Guthrie Smith and John Oswald Mitchell, 1878

133 Young Family Collection

134 Western District Cricket Union

135 Young Family Collection; Dumbarton Football Club

136 Young Family Collection; Wikipedia

137 Scottish Post Office Directories 1773 to 1911

138 Young Family Collection; Scottish Post Office Directories 1773 to 1911; Kilmarnock Football Club

139 Vale of Leven Football Club; Young Family Collection

140 Scottish Post Office Directories 1773 to 1911; Young Family Collection

141 Scottish Post Office Directories 1773 to 1911

142 Young Family Collection

143 Young Family Collection

144 Airdrieonians Football Club; Young Family Collection

145 Young Family Collection

146 Scottish Post Office Directories 1773 to 1911

147 Young Family Collection; Scottish Post Office Directories 1773 to 1911

148 Scottish Post Office Directories 1773 to 1911; Young Family Collection

149 Young Family Collection; Scottish Post Office Directories 1773 to 1911

150 Scottish Post Office Directories 1773 to 1911; Young Family Collection

151 Scottish Post Office Directories 1773 to 1911; Young Family Collection

152 Young Family Collection; Scottish Post Office Directories 1773 to 1911

153 Young Family Collection; Scottish Post Office Directories 1773 to 1911

154 Scottish Post Office Directories 1773 to 1911; Young Family Collection

155 Scottish Post Office Directories 1773 to 1911; Young Family Collection

156 Young Family Collection

157 St. Johnstone Football Club; Young Family Collection

158 Hugh Barrow - Glasgow Academicals Rugby Football Club; Scottish Post Office Directories 1773 to 1911; Young Family Collection

159 Scottish Football Museum at Hampden

160 Young Family Collection; Wikipedia

161 Scottish Post Office Directories 1773 to 1911; Young Family Collection

162 Scottish Post Office Directories 1773 to 1911; Mitchell Library Glasgow

163 TR Annan & Son - Glasgow in Panorama 1907; Young Family Collection

165 East Dunbartonshire Council Photo Library; Young Family Collection

166 Young Family Collection

167 Young Family Collection

168 Young Family Collection

169 Young Family Collection

170 Young Family Collection

171 Young Family Collection

172 Young Family Collection

173 Young Family Collection

178 The Royal Commission on the Ancient and Historical Monuments of Scotland

180 Crown copyright

182 Otago Daily Times, Issue 5236, 28th November 1878
183 Otago Daily Times, Issue 5236, 28th November 1878
192 The Bailie, 15 October 1890
193 Young Family Collection
194 Young Family Collection
196 Young Family Collection
197 Young Family Collection
198 Young Family Collection
199 Fifty Years Reminiscences of Scottish Cricket – David Drummond Bone, 1898
203 Aston Villa Player - Archie Hunter 1879 -1890 Photo 6″x4″ Reprint
204 Wikipedia
217 Young Family Collection
218 Young Family Collection
219 Young Family Collection